JUDSON PRESS

I'm a Piece of Work!
SISTERS SHAPED BY GOD

Cynthia L. Hale

Edited by Kathryn V. Stanley

JUDSON PRESS
PUBLISHERS SINCE 1824
VALLEY FORGE, PA

I'm a Piece of Work! Sisters Shaped by God
© 2010 by Judson Press, Valley Forge, PA 19482-0851

Library of Congress Cataloging-in-Publication Data

Hale, Cynthia L.
I'm a piece of work! : sisters shaped by God / Cynthia L. Hale ; edited by
Kathryn V. Stanley. -- 1st ed. p. cm.
Includes bibliographical references (p.   ).
ISBN 978-0-8170-1571-8 (pbk. : alk. paper) 1. Christian women--Religious
life. 2. African American women--Religious life. 3. Self-realization--Religious
aspects--Christianity. I. Stanley, Kathryn V. II. Title.

                                                       BR563.N4H335 2010
248.8'4308996073--dc22
2009038531

Printed in the U.S.A.

First Edition, 2010.

Contents

Who Are We?

Who are we?
We are black. We are brown.
We are ebony. We are ivory.
We are dark, medium brown.
Slightly tanned, we are light.

We are tall, stately, well-built.
Not so well-built.
We are short and fat.
A little or a lot, overweight, out of shape.

Who are we?
We are beautiful, average looking,
hardly noticeable, or so we think.
Our hair is long and silky.
Our hair is naturally or "soft and free" curly.
Our hair is nappy.

Who are we?
We are happy; we are sad,
We are sensitive, gentle, we are mad.
We laugh, we cry,
experience pain, ecstasy, joy.

We are powerful,
in control, we can handle anything!
No, we can't! We are not in control.
We are timid, sometimes shy, insecure, often afraid!

Who are we?
We are the life of the party.
Ain't no party 'til we get there!
Everybody likes us. No, they don't.
No one seems to like me. In fact,
There are times when I don't even like myself!

Who are we?
We are successful, and we are struggling.
We want to achieve, but it's not easy.
We are lawyers and doctors, judges and engineers,
homemakers, preachers, administrators, teachers.
We are retired, unemployed, on welfare, don't care.

We are married, single, divorced, unattached and looking.
We are wives and mothers, daughters, aunts, cousins.
We are sisters and girlfriends.

Who are we?
We are women, fearfully and wonderfully made,
created in God's own image and likeness.
"So God created human beings in his own image,
in the image of God created he them,
male and female created he them."

We are women.
The very essence of power and majesty
endowed with the attributes of beauty
gentleness, love, a sensitive nature,
and an understanding heart.

We are the inspiration
the world over for story,
song, poem, and painting alike.

Who are we?
We are women.
Our legacy is great;
our spiritual heritage is greater.
We are Sarah who gave birth to a nation
even though she was way past her childbearing years.
We are Esther, a peasant girl who became a Persian queen
at such a time as God needed her to save his people.
We are Naomi and Ruth, Deborah and Hulda
        Mary and Martha.

We comforted our lord, gave him birth,
washed his feet, and anointed his head with oil.
We were last at the cross, first at the tomb,
first to tell of the resurrection, and it was our quiet
but strong faith that caused us to reach out,
touch the hem of his garment, and be healed.

We were present at the first prayer meeting on Pentecost.
We were the first European convert.
We colabored with Paul and the other apostles
in turning the world upside down.
Who are we?
We are women, fearfully and wonderfully made.
Marvelous are God's works,
    and that my soul knows right well.

Introduction

I have a confession to make that I am not very proud of. Ready? I spent the first forty-plus years of my life trying to discover who I am. I may have seemed to have had it all together, but that was not the case. If only I had known who the real me was sooner, I could have accomplished so much more by now. I would have started living a freer, more emotionally fulfilling life long before now. I would be truly devastated if it weren't for the fact that I firmly believe that God redeems and restores the wasted times of our lives.

I now know that self-discovery is a lifelong process and that we all are a work in progress. But I don't believe that the process has to take as long for you as it took for me. Whether you will admit it or not, like me, some of you are taking too much time discovering who you are. Like me, you need to be free from all the baggage that weighs you down and holds you back. You need to discern and dismiss the distractions that are keeping you from reaching your destiny.

Not knowing who you are has a number of drawbacks. One is lack of self-assurance and self-confidence. When we do not fully affirm our dignity and worth and uniqueness, we tend to think less highly of ourselves than we ought, and we come across as insecure. I'm sure I'm not the only one who has ever felt this way.

When we are not confident about who we are, we also tend to second-guess ourselves, even when we know what we are talking about and know what we are doing. We tend to downplay our abilities and are afraid to reveal our true level of giftedness, intelligence, and insightfulness. We can't see just how powerful and persuasive, dynamic and determined, intuitive and influential we really are. And we don't want anyone else to see either.

Instead of being our true selves, we play a role that fits others' expectations of us and allows them to be comfortable with us. We try not to come across as intimidating, and we want to ensure everyone else's happiness, even if we are miserable.

Some of us even think that being true to ourselves is selfish and unspiritual or a betrayal of the people we love and our responsibility to them. We worry that they will disapprove of or abandon us.

Another danger of not knowing who we are is the tendency to settle for less than we deserve. We make few, if any, demands in our relationships. We just go along to get along, whether in intimate relationships, on our jobs, at school, or even in the church.

If I had known who I am earlier in life, I would not have chosen to become involved in some of the relationships I entered, with men especially. For years, I didn't realize that I needed someone in my life secure enough to handle me. Someone to affirm my dignity and worth, someone who could encourage me, build me up, someone who was on his way somewhere, so that he could help me get to where I was going and not try to hold me back. Someone who was up for the challenge rather than constantly defining me as controlling, pushy, aggressive, opinionated, and mouthy. I know I'm a piece of work! The question is, Can you handle me?

When we are unsure of who we are, we also allow others to define us. In our relationships, we tend to do and to be whatever anyone needs us or wants us to be. We dance to everyone else's tune and are then frustrated when no one dances to ours.

But there comes a time in our lives when we come to ourselves and say, "Enough is enough!" There comes a time when we realize that others cannot define us, because who we are is much more than they could ever imagine. There comes a time when we start knowing who we are, because we begin to see ourselves through the eyes of Whose we are. No one knows us better than God. No one has the right to define us but God. After all, God designed us. God shaped us for significance and destined us for greatness! Yes, we are pieces of work—created in the image of the most high God.

I have been given a ministry of ensuring that all of God's daughters embrace themselves and the calling that God has placed on their lives. Far too many of us have allowed fears and insecurities to rob us of the desires of our own hearts and to rob the world of our God-given gifts and abilities. It's time for us to take back everything we have given away trying to be less than God made us. It's time we allow God to shape us into the pieces of work we are created to be. It is my prayer that these pages will help you begin the wonderful journey of becoming the woman—the piece of work—God shaped you to be. While not intentionally autobiographical, these pages reflect my own struggle to break free from internal insecurities and low self-esteem, as well as from the expectations and opinions of others that kept me from being all God created and designed me to be.

It is my prayer that you will become the daughter of destiny God created you to be, that you will no longer settle for anything less than God's best for your life, and that you will learn to speak words of hope that will shape the lives of other women whom God places in your path.

Shaped for Significance

O LORD, you have searched me and known me.
You know when I sit down and when I rise up;
    you discern my thoughts from far away.
You search out my path and my lying down,
    and are acquainted with all my ways.
Even before a word is on my tongue,
    O LORD, you know it completely.
You hem me in, behind and before,
    and lay your hand upon me.
Such knowledge is too wonderful for me;
    it is so high that I cannot attain it.

Where can I go from your spirit?
    Or where can I flee from your presence?
If I ascend to heaven, you are there;
    if I make my bed in Sheol, you are there.
If I take the wings of the morning
    and settle at the farthest limits of the sea,
even there your hand shall lead me,
    and your right hand shall hold me fast.
If I say, "Surely the darkness shall cover me,
    and the light around me become night,"
even the darkness is not dark to you;
    the night is as bright as the day,
    for darkness is as light to you.

For it was you who formed my inward parts;
    you knit me together in my mother's womb.
I praise you, for I am fearfully and wonderfully made.
    Wonderful are your works; that I know very well.
My frame was not hidden from you,
    when I was being made in secret,
    intricately woven in the depths of the earth.
Your eyes beheld my unformed substance.

In your book were written all the days
that were formed for me,
when none of them as yet existed.
How weighty to me are your thoughts, O God!
How vast is the sum of them!
I try to count them—they are more than the sand;
I come to the end—I am still with you.

Search me, O God, and know my heart;
test me and know my thoughts.
See if there is any wicked way in me,
and lead me in the way everlasting.
—Psalm 139:1-18, 23-24

The Courage to Be the Real You

Psalm 139:13-16

At some point in our lives, all of us have struggled with becoming our true selves. This struggle is a difficult one, because often we don't even know who we are supposed to be. People around us work hard at dictating who they think we should be and try to squeeze us into their molds. The world confuses us by encouraging us to be like everyone else—to wear what everyone else is wearing, style our hair like everyone else, or paint our nails a certain way. Some of us go along with the program, even when something on the inside tells us it doesn't quite fit.

The Great Cover-up

Our quest to fit in often leaves us feeling left out. Our self perceptions are deeply rooted in how we compare to worldly standards. As a result, we find it difficult to embrace the woman in the mirror. Our hair is not the right texture, our skin is the wrong tone, our lips are too thick, our hips are too broad, our busts are either too big or not big enough. We detest our protruding stomachs, our sagging butts, and our thunder thighs. The media is often our mirror for the way we think we should look. And, if we don't meet the media's standard, some of us feel downright ugly. So we compare ourselves to others, like that actress in our favorite movie or tv show. We wish we were like them instead of embracing the beauty and mystique that is uniquely ours. We use a variety of wardrobe accessories and cosmetics to cover up who we really are.

Some of us also try to cover up who we are on the inside. We feel that being popular or accepted is more important than being ourselves. From an early age, we learn to be what other people want or expect us to be. If your mother never became the doctor she dreamed of being, she may expect you to become a doctor, even though you cannot stand the sight of blood. A teacher may encourage you to take a particular direction in life, even if that direction is not in keeping with your gifts and passions. You don't want to disappoint the people who have loved and supported you. No one feels good about going against the wishes of well-meaning people who just want what is "best." So you may try to please everyone around you. Now you may be feeling miserably trapped by others' expectations, with seemingly no way out.

Consumed by Others

Our attempts to express our individualities often fail because we become consumed with other people's opinions. We allow disapproving comments about the genuine us to put us back into our boxes. I have experienced this personally.

I like bright colors, especially red. When I was in seminary, I went home dressed in a red suit, with my nails and lips painted to match. I just knew I was looking good. But when I stopped by my grandmother's house, she expressed disapproval of what I was wearing, because she believed that a preacher shouldn't wear red. She compared me to a Jezebel! I know she didn't mean any harm, but after that incident, I began wearing more conservative colors so that I wouldn't offend anybody. It was important to me to dress the part of a "good" preacher. I bought into the notion that to be a preacher, I had to lose my unique sense of style.

We women often struggle with being the real us when it comes to our intimate relationships. If you are trying to attract, date, or marry someone, you may become someone other than you are to make him happy. If he's into football, you may acquire a taste for football or at least pretend while you sit there bored stiff. If he expects you to be quiet and demure, you may stuff your oversized personality into a safe place, hoping that it will not burst loose before the appropriate time. If he's the extrovert, you may pretend to enjoy the large get-togethers even though you would rather stay at home. Many of us feel that if we are too "this" or "that" we will scare men away. At times we may portray ourselves as being less intelligent than we are and may behave as if we are less gifted or capable. We may even apologize for being bold, brassy, large, and in charge, tight and usually right. We may apologize for expressing ourselves truthfully and directly. We may end up miserable and unhappy in a relationship or angry and depressed because we are not in one, because we have tried unsuccessfully to fit into the mold of other people's expectations.

A Unique Design

Despite everything around us that tells us we are not okay just as we are, there is good news for you and me! We were designed and intended to be unique individuals. More than that, it is ultimately easier to be the unique person you were designed to be than it is to try to be like someone else or what someone else wants or expects you to be.

Our fingerprints bear scientific witness to our uniqueness. But we are unique in other ways, too. No one else has the style, class, sassiness, sexiness, and mystique that you possess. No one else points her finger, purses her lips, puts her hands on her hips, and lets her backbone slip like you. Most importantly, no one else has been designed with the destiny, plan, and purpose that God has for you. You are somebody special. Did you ever think that God made you who you are for such a time as this? God needs someone with your strength, your intellect, your intuition to help people who are without direction and vision find their way.

What would happen if you danced to a tune other than what is accepted or expected? What would happen if we all got to the place where we stopped trying to fit into a mold? What if making other people happy fell from the top of our agendas? Let's test it out! I say that we set a date and time when we take off our masks and make it clear to everyone—including us—that we're finally going to be real! How about starting today?

But how do you begin to discover the real you when for so long you have been in hiding? You may even be so accustomed to hiding your true self that you would not even recognize your true self if she slapped you in the face. How, then, do you begin to reconnect your current persona with the person whom God made you to be? You need some tools to begin this journey to the real you, and I have just the thing.

See Yourself through God's Eyes

The only way we can embrace our true selves is to return to the One who designed us to be who we are. You see, God is the only one who can define us, because God designed us. God's opinion is the only one we can really trust, because God is the one who created us. Not only did God create us, but God created us in the divine image! That means that when we see ourselves through God's eyes, we see the beauty and majesty of our Creator reflected right back.

> Then God said, "Let us make humankind in our image, according to our likeness; and let them have dominion over the fish of the sea, and over the birds of the air, and over the cattle, and over all the wild animals of the earth, and over every creeping thing that creeps upon the earth." So God created humankind in his image, in the image of God he created them; male and female he created them (Genesis 1:26-27).

When creating human beings, God made a mirror image of God's self. Therefore, we were created to make God known in all the earth. Like God, we can think thoughts great or small, and we have the ability to reason. We can make plans, distinguish between right and wrong, relate to others, love, and feel. God made us for relationship with God's self. Scripture reminds us of the special position we have in relationship to God and to God's creation:

> When I look at your heavens, the work of your fingers, the moon and the stars that you have established; what are human beings that you are mindful of them, mortals that you care for them? Yet you have made them a little lower than God, and crowned them

with glory and honor. You have given them dominion over the works of your hands; you have put all things under their feet. (Psalm 8:3-6)

When God created us, God created something extraordinary. Even the second account of creation shows us just how special we are as women. You see, God created us from one of Adam's ribs. So, God saved the best for last! We were created with dignity and great worth! God sets us apart. When we realize that we were not only created by God, but we are created in God's own image, we can take an entirely new perspective on who we are as women. The sky is the limit for what we can become.

Keeping the Reflection Clear

I want to revisit the area of intimate relationships, because that is where many of us tend to lose ourselves, even after we have come to know who we are. Married women tend to interpret improperly the idea of two becoming one flesh to mean that, once we are married, we are no longer our own person. That could not be further from the truth. Marriage brings together two distinct individuals with their own personalities, styles, likes and dislikes, gifts and abilities to enhance the lives of one another. Marriage is intended to be a complementary relationship, that allows both partners to pursue their own purpose and walk in their own destiny. If you lose yourself totally in another, how can you provide a perspective that is helpful to him? How can you help each other become the best you can be?

It is important for us to remember that, even when we are joined with another, we continue to be a distinct person created in God's image and likeness. And, while we are all created in the image and likeness of God, we are not all just alike. We each have a unique brand. Psalm 139 attests to our uniqueness.

Celebrating Our Uniqueness

God created each of us with divine intention. God knew exactly the kind of person you would need to be to fulfill the purpose for which you were created. God gave you the personality for the purpose for which you have been created. Whether you are bold,

I'm a Piece of Work!

brassy, quiet, or quirky, God blessed you with unique personality traits to fulfill the task. You are intellectually equipped for the job. You are spiritually equipped for every good work. You are shaped for significance and made for ministry.

So instead of looking down on ourselves because of who we aren't or who we wish we were or who others want us to be, we need to do as the psalmist did and praise God, because we are "fearfully and wonderfully made." Sing praise for the women God made us to be from head to toe, inside and out, flaws, imperfections, and all.

The Hebrew word for *fearfully* is *yare,* which means to be feared, to be reverenced, to terrify, or to make afraid. Here we are, afraid ourselves when we are to be feared. Some of us are afraid of what others may think or say about us. Let them talk. In fact, give them something to talk about with your fine, foxy, and fabulous self. God has made you fearfully. You are to be held in awe and highly esteemed. Don't you know how "dangerous" you are? Be who you are. Don't hold anything back. Stop walking around with your head hung down and your shoulders stooped. Hold your head up high. Keep your back straight and shoulders erect. Walk like you know who you are and where you are going.

Not only has God made you fearfully, God has also made you wonderful and marvelous. The root of the Hebrew word for *marvelous* is the word *pala.* It means to be distinguished, to be extraordinary, to be wonderful, to be astonishing. This word is typically used to describe God. Yet fifteen times in Scripture, the word *pala* is used to refer to human beings. Yes, you and me. Well, it makes perfect sense. Since God is fearful and wonderful, it stands to reason that those who are made in God's image are fearful and wonderful, too! You are extraordinary!

Embrace God's Vision of the Real You

Once you begin to see yourself through God's eyes, you can develop the courage to be the real you. Your attitude will begin to reflect that you are a woman wonderfully and fearfully made in God's image. You will no longer allow the world to squeeze you into its mold. You will be able to celebrate and accept all of who you are, the good and the bad, knowing that through your weaknesses God's strength is made perfect. Does the fact that we see ourselves as wonderful right now mean we don't have things we want to improve upon? Of course not! Yet once you accept who God made you to be, you are better able to see the "you" you want to become.

When we wallow in our weaknesses or attempt to be all things to all people, we can easily lose sight of the vision that God has given us for our own lives. But when we embrace who God made us to be and begin to walk in the vision that God has given us, we begin to ask questions, such as, "What do I want to accomplish in life?" as opposed to "What do others want me to be?" We ask, "What brings me joy?" instead of "What pleases others?"

Feeling the Power

Once you have embraced the vision that God has given for your life, you must believe also that, through the gift of the Holy Spirit, you have been empowered to make the vision a reality. See yourself as powerful! The Holy Spirit gives us power, "for God did not give us a spirit of cowardice, but rather a spirit of *power* and of love and of self-discipline" (2 Timothy 1:7, emphasis added). It is important for you not only to see who you can become, but to know that you are empowered to become what you see.

Being the real you will take courage. People around you may not be comfortable with the real you. You may not be comfortable yourself. Who does she think she is? She's changing? Their discomfort may lead them to push you away. But those who truly love you will allow you the freedom to come out of your box, even if they have to adjust. There will be some people in your sphere of influence who have been waiting for you to step out, so they can step out and be real, too. They need a godly example of a courageous and powerful woman who is willing to throw caution to the wind and risk everything to become all that God created and destined her to be.

Taking Baby Steps

Taking small, seemingly insignificant steps may be just what you need to do in order to debut the real you. For me, one of those steps was my style of dress. Remember when I said that for years after my grandmother chastised me for wearing red, I changed my style of dress to a more conservative style? Well, years later a friend told me that she thought that my clothing style did not match my bold and brilliant personality. She confirmed something that I had been thinking. Today I allow the bold and brilliant personality that God gave me to be reflected in every aspect of my life, including my clothes.

You, too, can take small steps that reflect the real you. It may start with a jazzy new haircut or with speaking your mind in a setting when you would normally keep quiet. You may have to push past nagging inner voices that try to convince you not to take a positive step in becoming you. But push on, girl. Have the courage to press past your fears. Be bold enough to move ahead with your plans in spite of your fears. Continue to reveal more of the real you wherever you go, in whatever you are doing. It may seem strange at first, but sooner or later you will just do it naturally. You will reach a place where you cannot help being anything or anyone else but you. "God said to Moses, 'I AM WHO I AM' " (Exodus 3:14). God says to you, "You are who you are! I made you! You are mine! Now go show the world the wonderful and fearful woman you are!" Now go on, go!

A Brand-New Woman!

Ephesians 4:20-24

In Christ, we have been made new. The old has gone; the new has come! Yet this new life that we have been given in Christ is not meant to be static. We don't have the luxury of getting saved and simply finding ourselves a comfortable pew in the church where we can sit, thinking God expects nothing else of us.

Being born again is only the beginning. After we become new, we need to act new. That is what the apostle Paul told the Christians in Ephesus:

> That is not the way you learned Christ! For surely you have heard about him and were taught in him, as truth is in Jesus. You were taught to put away your former way of life, your old self, corrupt and deluded by its lusts, and to be renewed in the spirit of your minds, and to clothe yourselves with the new self, created according to the likeness of God in true righteousness and holiness. (Ephesians 4:20-24)

Did you know the goal of the Christian life is perfection? In Matthew 5:48, Jesus says that we are to "be perfect, therefore, as [our] heavenly Father is perfect." But used here, *perfection* doesn't mean "without fault." Rather, *perfection* in the Greek is *telious*, referring to wholeness and completion.

When you are perfect in this sense, you lack nothing in your character; you are all that God created and destined you to be. When you are perfect, you are no longer broken. When you are perfect, you are at your best. When you become perfect, you have reached full maturity in Christ and become clothed in all that he is (Romans 13:14).

Positioned for Perfection

When we accepted Christ, we were put in position to reach perfection. However, there are some practical things that we must do to bring out our best. To this end, Paul's letter to the Philippians provides guidance on how we can become brand-new women in Christ.

While writing the letter to the church at Philippi, Paul must have been contemplating how overwhelming the mere thought of perfection can be. In all honesty, it is rather overwhelming to think that we could ever become all that Christ is, especially when we consider who we are, where we have been, and what we have done. But Paul makes clear that we do not become perfect overnight:

> Not that I have already obtained this or have already reached the goal; but I press on to make it my own, because Christ Jesus has made me his own. Beloved, I do not consider that I have made it my own; but this one thing I do: forgetting what lies behind and straining forward to what lies ahead, I press on toward the goal ... in Jesus Christ. (Philippians 3:12-14)

Prescription for Perfection

In this passage, Paul provides a prescription for achieving perfection. Even after several years of being saved, Paul was able to admit that he was not perfect. And, while he was not all that he ought to be, he was on his way. Using the words *press, strain,* and *goal,* Paul compares the Christian life to a long-distance footrace, the ultimate finish line being full maturity in Christ. For Paul, the Christian life was a series of progressive steps that moved him closer to the goal. As with Paul, every step we take with Jesus brings us closer and closer to wholeness and is essential to bringing out the best in us.

Forget the Past
If you want to bring out the best in you, you have to get rid of the worst in you. Therefore, in his prescription for perfection,

Paul instructs us first of all to forget what is behind. Forget the past! Let it go!

We all have done things in the past that we are not proud of. We all have made some mistakes in life, gotten caught up in some situations, exercised poor judgment, made bad decisions, and done some things we regret. Truth be told, whether we like to admit it or not, some of us still struggle with old attitudes and behaviors. Paul articulates our struggle this way: "For I do not do the good I want, but the evil I do not want is what I do" (Romans 7:19).

Some of us don't want to admit our continuing struggle with sin. Others of us are still guilt-ridden and burdened by our past failures and indiscretions. As a result, we allow our pasts to render us ineffective in the present and to threaten to ruin our futures. If you can't seem to move away from your old stuff, then you can't claim all the blessings and opportunities God has for you, because you are convinced that you don't deserve them. You may think that no one who has been addicted, has committed adultery, has had an abortion, has lied, cheated, stolen, or has been as irresponsible and reckless as you have been deserves God's favor.

You may be paralyzed by the fear that someone will discover who you really are and what you have done. You may stay hidden in the shadows of your past, afraid to emerge into a bright new day. You may be ashamed and feel condemned before God, and you may not think that God can do anything great with your life. You may think that you have messed up so badly, failed so miserably, that there is no hope of your ever being successful.

I have a recommendation for all of you who have made some mistakes and made a mess of your lives, for all of you who are living with guilt, shame, regrets, and fear so that your past makes you useless to God: Forget it! Let it go! Move on!

Forgive Yourself

Jesus died on the cross for our sins. He declared us not guilty, forgiven, and pardoned. Now you must consider yourself not guilty, forgiven, and pardoned. "There is therefore now no condemnation for those who are in Christ Jesus" (Romans 8:1).

You are holding on to guilt for sin that has been forgiven and to condemnation for crimes that have already been expunged. Don't you know that you are a brand-new woman? It's time to forgive yourself!

> So if anyone is in Christ, [she] is a new creation: everything old has passed away; see, everything has become new! All this is from God who reconciled us to himself through Christ, and has given us the ministry of reconciliation; that is, in Christ God was reconciling the world to himself, not counting [women's] trespasses against them. (2 Corinthians 5:17-19)

You need to act new and stop beating yourself up over your past life. That stuff is dead, so bury it.

The residue from your past is like an old woman who likes to hang around to see if you will let her back in to take control again. You can move, change your address and telephone numbers, and leave nothing behind to trace. Yet, every now and then, that old woman shows up. The ole girl is always trying to reclaim her old position in your life. But don't be fooled by her tricks, because she has no real power over you anymore. She has lost all position in your life.

You have the power to make healthy and holy choices, to live a life that is clean, sober, holy, and victorious every day. And, if at anytime you fail, "if we confess our sins, he who is faithful and just will forgive us our sins and cleanse us from all unrighteousness" (1 John 1:9). If God can forgive us, who are we to hold a grudge against ourselves?

You see, forgiveness is so awesome. *To forgive* is literally to send away, to dismiss, to be done with, to let go of, to be released from the penalty and power of. When God forgives, God literally sends our sins away. God removes our sins from us as far as the east is from the west. When God forgives, God blots out our transgressions and remembers our sins no more. Isaiah 44:22 says, "I have swept away your transgressions like a cloud, and your sins like mist." If God doesn't condemn us, why should we condemn ourselves? We need to forgive ourselves and move on.

Renew Yourself

Becoming a new creation in Christ requires radically reordering the way we think and live. Remember what Paul says: "You were taught to put away your former way of life, your old self, corrupt and deluded by its lusts, and to be renewed in the spirit of your minds, and to clothe yourselves with the new self, created according to the likeness of God in true righteousness and holiness" (Ephesians 4:22-24). Think of it as purging your wardrobe!

Now that you are putting the old behind you, you have got to do things differently. In order to do things differently, you have to think differently; your attitude has to be made new. In order to renew yourself, you have to think new and then follow through by putting on the new self that is truly righteous and holy like God. Paul breaks it down this way:

> So then, putting away falsehood, let all of us speak the truth to our neighbors, for we are members of one another. Be angry but do not sin; do not let the sun go down on your anger, and do not make room for the devil. Thieves must give up stealing; rather let them labor and work honestly with their own hands, so as to have something to share with the needy. Let no evil talk come out of your mouths, but only what is useful for building up, as there is need, so that your words may give grace to those who hear. And do not grieve the Holy Spirit of God, with which you were marked with a seal for the day of redemption. Put away from you all bitterness and wrath and anger and wrangling and slander, together with all malice, and be kind to one another, tenderhearted, forgiving one another, as God in Christ has forgiven you. (Ephesians 4:25-32)

The things that we say and the ways that we say them must change if we are to be new. We can no longer make our points by degrading and tearing people down with words. Our words must be truthful and kind. It is not what we say, but the way we say it that often causes problems. Our nonverbal communication is often as bad as our verbal communication—the way we shake our fingers in people's faces, roll our eyes, poke our lips out when we don't get our way. Sisters, this is not our best! It is time for us to mature to new levels in Christ. If you are to become a brand-new woman, you must walk and talk in a new way.

Forgive Others

Not only do we need to put our sins and shortcomings behind us; we also need to put away the hurts, the disappointments, and the situations that are impeding our progress, those things that someone else might have done to us. You may find it hard to forget some of the things that have been done to you or the people who have done them. I understand, because I have been there. Several years ago, I was so consumed with anger and bitterness from things that people had said and done to me that I would "go off" with the slightest provocation. The bitterness that had built up inside of me would erupt like a volcano with little notice. God told me to forgive and forget. I told God I would forgive, but I would never forget. I did not want to forget. How could I forget? Besides, I didn't want to let the people who had wronged me off the hook that easily. I was afraid they might think they could try to hurt me again.

In Scripture, the word *forget* refers to obliterating the memory of the past. When God says in Hebrews 10:17, "I will remember their sins and their lawless deeds no more," God does not mean that God literally forgets our sins. God never forgets anything. God cannot forget. After all, God knows everything there is to know about anything. What God means by *forget* is that God will no longer be affected or influenced by our sins. God will not treat us as our sins deserve, nor will God hold them against us. Our sins will no longer affect our standing with God.

With us, forgetting the past is to no longer allow it to affect or influence our lives. By putting the past behind, you no longer allow it to have any power over you. We must confront ghosts of the past, things that leave us with haunting memories. Every day, many of us live with, work with, and go to class or even church with people who have hurt us deeply. The memory of the pain they caused may seem unforgivable and unforgettable. But whatever has happened should not continually keep you from going on with your life. We need to forgive others so that we can move on.

God forgives our sins and heals our hurts. God is *Jehovah-Rapha'*, the God who heals us, who picks up the broken pieces of our lives and hearts, and who allows us to move forward. You cannot change the past, but you do not have to allow it to have the power to affect your emotions, dictate your decisions and choices, influence your future, and hinder your progress. We are on our way to becoming brand-new women! If the Holy Spirit is to move us to a new level in our relationship with God and with others, we have to let go of the pain, anger, and bitterness that bind us.

Hebrews 12:1 states, "Therefore, since we are surrounded by so great a cloud of witnesses, let us also lay aside every weight and the sin that clings so closely, and let us run with perseverance the race that is set before us." If we are to run our life's journey as this text instructs, then we are going to have to travel light. You cannot reach new levels if you are weighed down with a whole bunch of baggage.

Be clear that everything that hinders is not necessarily bad in and of itself. What makes it bad is that it is something that holds us back and impedes our progress or covers up the best in us. Your current relationship may not be a bad one, but it may not be a good one either. He may not be a bad person; he just may not the right person for you. He may not be God's best for you. Your current job may not be a bad one, but it may not be a good one either. It may not be a bad salary or a bad work environment, but it may not be God's best for you.

You may be thinking that someone is better than no one and something is better than nothing. With that mind-set, you may be settling for less than you deserve. If the something is going nowhere, then neither are you. It might be time to leave that job or relationship behind! But don't be discouraged. Forgetting the past is only half of Paul's prescription for God's perfection in you!

Press On for the Prize

The second part of Paul's prescription for perfection may surprise you. You see, it isn't only our past failures, our past disappointments, our past hurts that we must put behind us. We are also called to leave behind our past triumphs and victories. Why? Like a job or a relationship that may be something but fall short of everything God has in mind, our past triumphs and victories are something—but not everything. God has more in store for us! If we truly want to move to a higher calling, we cannot rest on our laurels. We have to leave behind the accomplishments, achievements, and victories we have already attained. We have the next leg of our race to run!

Paul had achieved a lot in his life before he encountered the risen Christ on Damascus Road. Saul, as he was known back then, was a well educated, well positioned, wealthy man who had everything life could offer. Yet he gave it all up for the sake of knowing Christ. After he became a Christian, God blessed him in even greater ways than God had before. God allowed him to become the prince of preachers and a pastor par excellence. Given Paul's level of spiritual, intellectual, and educational achievement, it seems odd that he would say, "Not that I have already obtained this or have already reached the goal, but I press on to make it my own, because Christ Jesus has made me his own" (Philippians 3:12). Sisters, I do not consider myself to have taken hold of it. But one thing I do: forgetting what is behind, I *press on*.

Like Paul, some of you are living a fabulous life. You may have dealt with your past and may have reached a level of spirituality, prosperity, and success in life greater than you have ever known before. You may have grown spiritually in ways that you never imagined. When you look back over your life, you are amazed at God's grace and goodness. You may have been victorious through many hard trials. You may have overcome unbelievable odds to mature to where you are in Christ. When you consider how God made a way out of no way, it takes your breath away. You can hardly believe how good God has been to you.

Yet, when considering how far you have come, how richly you have been blessed, and how satisfying life is, you must not become self-satisfied and content. You must not think you have fully arrived. Even when you think you've reached your peak, there is always more! The best is yet to come! Even when you think you are at the top of your game, God raises the stakes. The standard for perfection is becoming all that Christ is. None of us is there yet. God is not finished with any of us.

Be on the Lookout

Believe it or not, as blessed as you may be, God is not through blessing you. Be on the lookout for the new thing God wants to do for and through you!

The prophet Isaiah said, "Do not remember the former things, or consider the things of old. I am about to do a new thing; now it springs forth, do you not perceive it? I will make a way in the wilderness and rivers in the desert" (Isaiah 43:18-19). The former things to which Isaiah referred were the ways that God had moved on Israel's behalf in the past. The fact that God had delivered them from four hundred years of slavery in Egypt, had brought them across the Red Sea, had drowned their enemies, and had taken them through forty years in the wilderness into the Promised Land is mind-blowing. Yes, God had blessed the people of Israel. But God said through the prophet, and God says to us, "Although that was something, you ain't seen nothing yet!" What God has for you, where God is trying to take you will blow your mind.

Whatever God says comes to pass. God's words become reality the moment they are spoken. Isaiah says, "Now it springs forth." The Scripture does not say tomorrow or next year, but now. Don't get stuck on what God did in the past, no matter how wonderful. Know that God has more wonderful things in store for you. Grab hold of what God has for you now.

Dare to Dream

We can perceive what God is leading us to do if we just dare to dream. Daydreaming is one of my favorite pastimes. During the day while driving, sitting at my desk, or attending a meeting, when I know I should be more attentive, sometimes I find myself carried away by a dream. I dream of what is possible in my life and ministry. Dreams are those strongly desired goals, distinctive hopes, and images dancing in your imagination, exciting you, stirring up your passions, setting your soul on fire, and unleashing energy within that is not easily contained.

What are your dreams? What visions are floating around in your head and heart? Every one of us has the ability to dream. To dream is a gift of God. We have the ability to make great dreams come true. We have the ability to see a vision and watch it come to pass. Each of us has at least one dream for our lives. Great things can happen when you follow your dreams. Dreams reveal to us the reason God created us. They are the God-sized potential and possibilities for our lives. Without a vision, it is not possible to see the good things God has for us. You can miss God's best by only perceiving what is visible.

Bringing out the best is daring to dream, to see a new you, and to then focus on becoming the woman you dared to dream of becoming. To focus is to bring all your energies, resources, and commitment to bear on the goal. The goal is bringing out the best of you in Christ Jesus. If you are going to bring out the best in you, you have to get serious about pursuing God and what God has for you.

Pursue God's Presence

Now that we are saved, we must take possession of that for which we have been possessed. To pursue something is to go after it, strain toward it, put all your effort into it, like a hunter pursuing game, like an Olympic runner going for the gold, straining every muscle, every fiber of her being. This is no time to casually stroll through life with no goals and ambitions. Too many of us have no real ambition, motivation, or passion. We wonder why our lives are so unfulfilling. We wonder why we are not experiencing the full joy of the life we are living in Christ. You may be living beneath your privilege by refusing to pursue all God has for you.

Pursuing God in Christ will bring out the best in you. Before Paul even talks about pressing toward his goal, he expresses a deep desire to know Christ: "I want to know Christ and the power of his resurrection and the sharing of his sufferings by becoming like him in his death, if somehow I may attain the resurrection from the dead" (Philippians 3:10-11).

Even before he found Christ, Paul had been a man of great passion and ambition. But he had the wrong ambitions and focused on the wrong things. When he met Jesus, his ambitions changed; he refocused his energies and reordered his steps. The more Paul focused on Christ and got to know him, the more Christlike he became. You see, our lives reflect who and what we focus our attention on. We start to look like and act like those with whom we spend our time.

Therefore, if we are to emerge as brand-new women in Christ, our chief ambition in life must be to pursue God and the things of God. We must study God's Word daily. We must stay in God's presence through daily prayer and meditation. As we pursue Christ, we can then know Christ. As we know Christ, we will become more like Christ. Through him, we are on our way to reaching perfection. Become new, my sister, and then press on!

A Kept Woman

Psalm 139:13-16

When I was a child, I would hear adults use the term *kept woman*. While I didn't know what the term meant, I was fascinated by it and asked my parents on several occasions what a kept woman was. Judging from their response or, rather, the lack thereof, it became obvious to me that a kept woman was something a little girl like me should not aspire to be. Quite honestly, though, knowing that it was inappropriate piqued my interest even more. A curious and precocious child, I just had to know what it was to be a kept woman. So I conducted my own research by eavesdropping on adult conversations, looking up the word *kept* in the dictionary and piecing the information together to develop my own definition of *kept woman*.

I determined that the word *kept* is the past tense of the verb "to keep," and that one meaning of that verb was to be tended to or taken care of. It entailed maintaining a thing in a good, fitting, and orderly fashion or condition. I concluded, then, that a kept woman is a woman who is maintained in a good, fitting, and orderly fashion. On that basis, I didn't understand why being a kept woman was something that my parents didn't want me to know about, let alone become. In my young mind, to be maintained in a good, fitting, and orderly fashion was a good thing. (I didn't understand that when people referred to a kept woman what they really meant was a woman who was financially supported by a lover, usually a married lover. Indeed, one of the synonyms for *kept woman* is *mistress*.)

Now that I am a little older, I still think being a kept woman is a good thing. In fact, I can unapologetically say that I am a kept woman. Based on what you know a kept woman to be, some of you would raise your eyebrows or look down your nose down at me. Many of you can't wait to put down this book fast enough to tell your friends that the Reverend Dr. Cynthia L. Hale is a kept woman. In fact, some of you would use even more colorful terms. Despite what anyone might think, I proudly admit to being a kept woman. Some of you are, too, and may not even know it!

You may already be the talk of the town. You have a special glow about you. You have never known such peace and joy, have never been loved like this before. Everyone may want to know why you are looking so fine, stepping so high, confident in ways you've never been before, strutting around as if you have a gold mine in your backyard, handling life's situations with the confidence with which you have never handled them before. Everyone you meet may want to know what in the world is going on with you. When people ask you what's going on with you, tell them that your life is the way it is today because you are being kept. Tell them you are a kept woman.

Kept by God

"Kept by whom?" they may ask. They may still assume that the one keeping you is somebody else's husband. So make it very clear to everyone around you who your Keeper is. Tell them, "My keeper is King of kings and LORD of lords; my keeper is El Shaddai, the All-Sufficient One, Adonai, El Elyon, the most high God. My keeper is the Alpha and the Omega, the beginning and the end. My keeper is Jehovah-Jireh, my provider; Jehovah-Shalom; my peace, Jehovah-Rapha, my healer; Jehovah-Tsidkenu, my righteousness. I stand complete in him. He's my everything; he keeps me alive! Tell them that the one who adores you, moves heaven and earth to see about you, and answers whenever you call is managing your affairs, bankrolling your dreams, and handling every detail of your life. Tell them that if they are not a "kept woman," they should want to be.

If haters still don't believe you and still try to make you the subject of gossip and innuendo, let me give you some tools from God's Word to put in your arsenal. In Psalm 139, the Lord reveals to us what it means to be kept. The book of Psalms is a collection of personal songs and poems that the Israelites used during corporate worship or for personal devotion. The Psalms provide guidance for developing a personal relationship with God. They teach us how to be honest with God and allow God to reveal God's self and become real in our lives. From the Psalms, we learn how to tell God our hurts and our hopes, joys and sorrows, while simultaneously meditating on God's goodness and glory. The Psalms encourage us to give God the praise God is so worthy to receive.

In Psalm 139, we see evidence of an intensely personal relationship between the psalmist, David, and God. This psalm is actually David's meditation and prayer through which he asserts who he is and what he means to God. Likewise, in this psalm, we can discover who we are and how valuable we are to God. This psalm shows us what it means to be a kept woman.

God Knows Her

First, God intimately knows a kept woman. God couldn't take care of us the way God does if God didn't know us. From the very first verse of this psalm, we see how intimately God knows God's children:

> O Lord, you have searched me and known me.
> You know when I sit down and when I rise up;
> > you discern my thoughts from far away.
> You search out my path and my lying down,
> > and are acquainted with all my ways.
> Even before a word is on my tongue,
> > O Lord, you know it completely. (Psalm 139:1-4)

The Hebrew word for "to know" used here, *yada*, refers to intimate knowledge of another. This is the kind of intimate knowing that should exist between a husband and a wife. When you know someone intimately, there are no secrets between you and that person. You can stand before them naked and unashamed and allow them to see the real you. The makeup has come off, literally and figuratively. There is no more trying to make a good impression. You are who you are.

Just as friends and spouses can share intimate relationships, God knows everything there is to know about us: the good, the bad, and the ugly. God knows our strengths and weaknesses, our moods and attitudes. God is aware of all the nasty stuff that we try so hard to keep under wraps. You know what I am talking about. You try so hard to be on your best behavior and then something or someone hits a nerve, and, oops, it all oozes out! God knows it all. God knows our past hurts and our hopes for the future. God knows all our secrets, even the ones we hesitate to record in our journals for fear that someone will find them and read them. God knows all the questions you are hoping your mother, spouse, or best friend will never ask so you won't be tempted to lie. You know the affairs, the abortions, and the unexplained absences. And, God knows, too! Nothing in our lives is secret to God.

God digs around in your heart and mind to uncover every hidden thing. God finds your insecurities and fears. God discovers the questions you have deep inside, such as, why the one you trusted betrayed you, why your father never came to see about you, why your mother died and left you, why no one has ever asked to marry you, why your husband is cheating on you, why no one is asking you out, or why you feel so rejected. God knows all of your questions and concerns, no matter how worldly and seemingly inappropriate your questions may be. God knows! The psalmist testifies that nothing escapes or goes unnoticed by God.

God Understands Her

How many times have you thought to yourself, *Nobody really knows me or understands what I've been through, what I'm going through right now, how I really feel?* People say they care, but sometimes we feel so alone in our pain, we wonder if anybody really does.

A woman kept by God doesn't have to worry about the fact that God knows her, because God also understands her. God loves and accepts us unconditionally. Even when we fall, God covers us and does not allow us to be exposed and doesn't hold it against it. Knowing how fragile we are, God handles us like a fine piece of china, trying to keep us from falling and shattering into a million pieces. And when we do fall, God is ready to forgive us if we just ask. God wipes the slate clean and disposes of our indiscretions. God picks up the broken pieces of our hearts and lives and puts them back together again.

God's intimate knowledge of us also means that God is sensitive to our needs. We never have to question whether God is saying and doing what is appropriate for us. God anticipates our every need. As women, we can't always understand why the special people in our lives behave as if they don't know what we need, when we need it, and how. We believe that, because they ought to know us so well, we shouldn't have to tell them what makes us happy or sad, makes us cry, or turns us on. I am sure you have chastised your husband or significant other for not knowing you well enough to say or do some things without your having to ask or tell.

It is true that intimate knowledge of another often exists between those who have an intimate relationship, especially if you've been together for a while. The truth of the matter is that it is not possible for any human to know everything there is to know about another, and those things they should know about us, they often don't. Sometimes your husband really doesn't know. Heaven only knows why he doesn't know. You have told him, your children have told him, the Holy Ghost has even told him. I'm not sure why it is, but I know that we women need to stop stressing about this reality, because it is what it is. Only God is omniscient, only God knows everything. Only God can anticipate all your needs. Only God never makes a mistake. Only God never forgets a date or misses a special occasion. God is always there when you are in need.

The psalmist says that only God perceives our thoughts, discerns our going out and our lying down, and is familiar with all our ways. God knows why we think what we think, do what we do, and say what we say. God understands us. God knit us together in our mothers' wombs. God knows intimately how we are wired.

God Holds On to Her

Remember when you thought you couldn't take anymore? Remember the time you said, "I'm through, and I'm out of here?" You were about to give up and walk away from it all. Remember when you were about to say or do something foolish but something kept you? You heard a sermon, a song, or even a kind word from a stranger. Then seemingly, out of nowhere, an unexplainable peace swept over you, an unspeakable joy flooded your soul, wisdom and understanding dropped into your spirit. You were left wondering, where did that come from?

Another mark of a woman who is kept by God is that God holds her close. God keeps one hand on her and does not let her too far out of sight. The psalm says:

> You hem me in, behind and before,
> and lay your hand upon me.
> Such knowledge is too wonderful for me;
> it is so high that I cannot attain it.
>
> Where can I go from your spirit?
> Or where can I flee from your presence?
> If I ascend to heaven, you are there;
> if I make my bed in Sheol, you are there.
> If I take the wings of the morning
> and settle at the farthest limits of the sea,
> even there your hand shall lead me,
> and your right hand shall hold me fast. (Psalm 139:5-10)

A kept woman has God's hands on her. Those incredibly strong and yet gentle and open hands bless us, provide for us, protect us, and hold us fast. When I was growing up, at times I would become anxious or get all bent out of shape about one thing or another. When this would happen, my daddy would gently place his hands on my head and assure me that everything would be all right. At other times, as we walked down a crowded street, when I felt the crowd pressing in on me and feared that I would be separated from him, my daddy would take my hand in his and guide me safely through the crowd. Though I'm a big girl now, every now and then, when life starts to press in on me, there are times when I long for strong hands to hold me tight. Knowing that we are held in the palm of God's hand and that, just like a daddy, God never lets go ought to give us great comfort and joy.

As women kept by God, we can know this: God will keep us even when we don't want to be kept! We are never out of God's sight, even when we try to run away from God. God gets too close for comfort for some of us, because God won't allow us to do what we want to do. So we try to put some distance between God and us so that we don't have to be accountable for our actions. But you should know by now that you can run, but you can't hide. Even if you try, you are never out of God's sight. Wherever we are, God is there, also. The psalmist says that even if we make our beds in Sheol or the place of the dead, God is even there.

We are kept even when we don't realize we need to be kept. God provides for us even before we recognize that we need God's intervention and provision. No matter where we find ourselves, emotionally, spiritually, as well as physically, God is there. God's sovereignty and care extend to wherever we are. God's presence cannot be limited to one place. God's authority and power cannot be contained. The Lord's hand will keep you wherever you are, even in the darkness, in those difficult places of discouragement and disappointment, in places where we feel afraid or lack confidence.

You may be discouraged about or fearful of a bad report from the doctor, a pink slip at work, the death of a loved one, or the future of a relationship. You may have been abused as a child or battered as an adult, and you haven't worked through all of that yet. Perhaps you never know when you will have a panic attack or when the pain will roll over you.

No matter what you have been or are going through, you have no reason to fear, because God is keeping you. Even when you feel as if you are dwelling in the darkest place of your life, know that God is there to shine a light upon you. Just walk in the Light. There is no need to be afraid of anything or anybody. If God is for you, who can be against you? You are a kept woman. God's hand is upon you. God has a hedge of protection around you. God has you covered!

This thought is almost too good to be true. That God would love us so, keeping us like only God can, anticipating and providing for our every need, is too wonderful to even comprehend. Why does God keep us the way God does? It's very simple: God made us, and we are valuable to God. David testifies to this fact:

> For it was you who formed my inward parts;
>> you knit me together in my mother's womb.
> I praise you, for I am fearfully and wonderfully made.
>> Wonderful are your works;
> that I know very well. (Psalm 139:13-14)

We were handmade, woven together in our mothers' wombs. The value of a handmade article far exceeds that of a mass-produced item because of the intricate detail. The same is true of us. We were not thrown together. God took great care in shaping us into masterpieces. You are tailor-made, fearfully and wonderfully put together, extraordinary! You were shaped for significance! Who wouldn't want to keep a woman like you? You're a keeper! And who wouldn't want to be kept by the awesome God who made us? God's a keeper!

God wants the world to know what can be done with a woman who is totally, undeniably kept! All I can do is paraphrase that contemporary psalmist James Cleveland and say, "Oh, that Jesus would keep me, keep me in his power divine!"

A Woman with Wings

Psalm 55:1-7

I love to fly (in an airplane, of course). I suppose my love for flying comes from the feeling of freedom and exhilaration I get soaring like a bird above the clouds. Flying makes me feel powerful, free from the cares of the world below. This is the case especially when I fly first class.

Yes, flying feels great, unless, of course, the plane happens to encounter turbulence. Not just a few bumps, but the kind of turbulence that causes the flight attendant to invite everyone to return to their seats; the kind that makes the pilot come over the intercom, stop all beverage service, and turn the FASTEN SEAT BELTS sign back on. The kind of turbulence that makes you feel as though you're riding a bronco. You feel out of control, especially of your feelings. Some of us just hold on for dear life and pray that God is not mad enough with anyone to allow the plane to fall out of the sky. Even those of us who think we have great faith have contemplated this faithless notion. I know I have.

Depending on the circumstances, there are times the pilot is able to take a plane that is experiencing turbulence to a higher altitude, transcending the rough air to a place where the air is smooth once again. Sometimes it even feels as if the bumps have helped to lift the plane to a higher altitude.

Encountering Turbulence

Life is a lot like flying. When the flight is smooth, we are carefree. Everything is copacetic; everything is going our way. We feel powerful, in control, able to handle anything and everything. At other times, it feels as though all hell has broken loose in our lives. We find ourselves in the midst of a crisis and don't know what to do. Turbulence has hit our lives, making the air around us rough. We no longer feel powerful. Instead, we feel helpless and sometimes hopeless.

Yes, life can be rough! It can be hard to handle at times. Everybody has issues, but we women seem to have more than our fair share. As a result, we experience particularly bad turbulence in our lives.

For some of us, health issues create turbulence. Sickness and disease sap our strength, threaten our sense of well-being, and diminish our quality of life. Aches, pains, and changes take place in our bodies as we get older. You may not be able to see as well as you used to. You may have to be a little more careful about what you eat and when. And gravity has caused certain body parts to head south.

Some of us encounter turbulence in our relationships. Maybe you have a man who doesn't always do what is right, so you think you may as well not have one. Maybe you don't have a man and you're wondering why. What's up with God? You've been delighting yourself in God, so why haven't you been given the desires of your heart (Psalm 37:4)?

Perhaps your children are causing the turbulence. You wonder when they are ever going to get it together. You love them and are glad you have them (most of the time), but there are those moments when you say to yourself, "If only I had known. What in the world was I thinking when I decided to become a parent?"

Issues from your childhood may cause turbulence. Maybe you were abused or neglected by one or both of your parents. You always wanted to be "Daddy's little girl," but your daddy was never around.

Or perhaps your father was in the house but was distant, mean, or unavailable to you emotionally and otherwise. Now that you are an adult, dealing with all the lingering emotions is more than you can stand.

You may be experiencing turbulence on your job. Maybe the job is really not challenging you. Someone with your intellect, skills, and abilities should be and could be doing so much more, but you feel stuck.

Your issue may be financial turbulence. Maybe your finances are shaky and you are wondering how you are going to make ends meet during this tough economic time. You may have an addiction to spending that you don't know how to kick. You keep buying things you don't need to try and fill a void in your life.

Tempted to Fly Away

Our issues, no matter what they are, create a turbulent battle within us. We're not sure how to respond. We may not even know how we will go on. When life gets rough, we seek solutions. And sometimes our first solution is to fly away. There are times when I have said to myself, "If I only had wings, I would fly away and be at rest. If I only had wings, I'd be out of here in a heartbeat." I know I'm not the only one who has felt like flying away sometimes.

How many times have you said to yourself, if I only had wings, I could fly away, out of range of the pain, above my circumstances, and be free from the chains that bind me? If I only had wings I would soar high like an eagle above the mess and madness, out of harm's way.

In Psalm 55, David affirms the desire to take flight when encountering life's pains:

"Oh, that I had the wings like a dove!
    I would fly away and be at rest;
truly, I would flee far away;
    I would lodge in the wilderness;
I would hurry to find a shelter for myself
    from the raging wind and the tempest. (Verses 6-8)

Some of you can relate to the psalmist at this very moment. You are looking for an escape, a place of refuge, someplace where you can forget your troubles and be at rest. You want to get away from the stress and the turmoil.

Like many of us, David was "going through." All he wanted was to get away. But when you're going through, seeking to get away is only a temporary solution. You can fly away for only so long before pain, trials, and tribulations catch up with you. Wherever we go, our pain lingers in our hearts, minds, and spirits. We can try and get away from our circumstances, but doing so does not provide a permanent solution.

Deciding to Fly Through

I would suggest to you that, instead of flying away, you should seek to fly through your circumstances toward a higher altitude, just as a pilot does when going through turbulence. Fly through it, not around it, over it, or under it! You must go through the rough spots to get whatever lesson God wants you to receive. Allow God to use turbulence to smooth out the rough places in your life. Allow God to deal with the issues you face decisively, to strengthen your mind and heart, which have grown weak and vulnerable. Allow God to use turbulence to give you the lift you need to soar to a new place in God.

Go through? you might be thinking. I've been going through for a long time. I'm tired of going through! I just want to be happy. I just want to be free. Know this: no matter what you are going through, if you have a relationship with Christ Jesus, you already are free. For if the Son sets you free, you are free indeed. So think free, and then live free.

We need to stop allowing the circumstances in our lives to continue to hold us in captivity. This is easier said than done, because breaking free isn't easy. When we look at our circumstances from a purely human perspective, things can be pretty discouraging. But things look a whole lot different from God's vantage point. We can only see things as they are right now, but God sees the end from the beginning. As Jeremiah 29:11 reminds us, God also has plans for us, plans to prosper us and not to harm us, plans to give us hope and a future. When we view the challenges of life from God's perspective, we see our challenges as possibilities and our problems as opportunities.

A Personal Example

Let me open a page from a difficult time in my own life. For many years, I was tormented by the fact that I have never been married. Though I appeared to be happy and content with my life, I really wasn't. I lived with a gnawing grief over the fact that God hadn't given me a husband and children. Though I had dated several men whom I believed were great prospects, none of them ever proposed marriage. The rejection I felt was difficult to handle. I just couldn't understand why God would leave me alone. I couldn't believe that no one wanted to marry me. As fine as I am (modest, too), I questioned my self-worth. My self-esteem plummeted. Wasn't I pretty, desirable, intelligent, and nice enough for someone to want to be my husband?

I decided to take matters into my own hands. I wanted a husband, and I was going to get one with or without God's help. So God turned me over to my own desires. And as you might imagine, the results were disastrous. A man came into my life who, I knew, wasn't the one God had for me. Nevertheless, I tried to make the relationship work. We did have lots of fun together, but he wasn't willing to make a commitment. I found myself trying to love a man who did not love me enough to commit. Since I did not have the strength to move on, I just kept hoping. And the more I hoped, the more I hurt. Finally, I had had enough. I knew I needed to end the relationship, but I couldn't gather the strength to let go, knowing that I would once again be alone. I was angry, hurt, and wanted to be bitter.

At some point, however, I realized that there might be something I needed to learn in this situation. The choice was mine to be bitter or become better. At some point in all our lives, we have to decide between bitterness and betterness. If we start asking, "Why me?" If we say, "How come things don't ever turn out the way I want them to?" we can become bitter with ourselves, with others, and even with God. On the other hand, if we view life's difficult moments as opportunities for personal and spiritual growth, then we can become better for ourselves, for others, and for God. Difficulties can provide the opportunity for God to mature us and work out the issues in our lives that keep us from being emotionally healthy and whole.

This was true in my case. Through this difficult relationship, I realized some things about myself. I was needy! I needed to be in relationships with certain people in order to feel good about myself. As a result, I would buy my friendships, picking up restaurant tabs, buying gifts, acting as the caretaker and nurturer in relationships. I did whatever I could to make the people in my life happy. I never wanted to displease anybody. Because I was insecure and had low self-esteem, I also needed others to validate me. Some of the persons I desired to be in relationship with didn't treat me as I deserved to be treated. But at the time, I didn't realize I deserved better.

I now know that God wanted to teach me to be my own person, to stand on my own two feet. I also needed to learn how to be content in my singleness. This required that I learn to trust God's love and to trust that God knows what is best and wants the best. I surrendered to God's perfect way in my life. I decided to allow God to use the process to mature me. I believe I could handle the problem a little better knowing that God had a purpose in allowing me to experience the pain, loneliness, and rejection. At the end of my brokenness, I knew there would be a blessing. While it didn't feel good, I believed that it was "all good" and that it would work for my good if I loved the Lord and let God be God (Romans 8:28). Knowing this, I decided to face my trials with joy!

Soaring on Wings of Joy

Joy? "I want to be happy," you might be saying. I wanted to be happy also, but the circumstances in my life at that point did not lend themselves to happiness. You see, happiness depends on what is happening. On the other hand, joy is the fruit of the Spirit that dwells on the inside. Joy is the presence of God inside of me. I could still have joy even in the midst of my trouble, because God remained inside me. The more I trusted God, the more joy I had. The more I submitted to God, the more joy I had. God's joy provided strength to elevate me above the clouds, above the turbulence of my circumstances. As I began to rejoice, I developed an intentional attitude of gratitude for what God was doing in my life.

There is reason to have joy in the midst of our troubles:

> Therefore, since we are justified by faith, we have peace with God through our Lord Jesus Christ, through whom we have obtained access to this grace in which we stand; and we boast in our hope of sharing the glory of God. And not only that, but we also boast in our sufferings, knowing that suffering produces endurance, and endurance produces character, and character produces hope, and hope does not disappoint us, because God's love has been poured into our hearts through the Holy Spirit that has been given to us (Romans 5:1-5).

God has a purpose for our sufferings. In this text, Paul makes clear that suffering can have value; pain can be productive. Suffering produces perseverance—the ability to handle pressure, to hang in there and not give up. If you don't ever go through anything, you will never develop the ability to handle the difficulties, pressures, and challenges that are all a part of life. When we make it through a difficult time, our character and confidence are strengthened, and we are better able to handle any and every new problem we encounter in the future.

That all sounds good, I know. But what do you need on a practical level to have joy while you're experiencing life's turbulence? First and foremost, you must pray without ceasing. An early-morning rendezvous with God allows you to begin your day joyfully. When you spend time in conversation with God, you are reminded of God's goodness. You are reminded that God is the source of your strength and that the joy of the Lord is, indeed, your strength.

Second, you must find what I call "praise points." Whenever you are about to give up or give in, whenever you are about to become bitter and angry, it is appropriate to acknowledge your feelings. But after acknowledging the pain, praise God, knowing that your nights might be full of weeping, but joy will come. Praise God knowing that any weapon formed against you will, ultimately, not prosper. Praise points are power points that provide the fuel you need to get through the turbulence.

Finally, you must study the Word of God. You may not feel like praising. You may not even feel like praying, but you can always read about the goodness of God, even if you can't feel it for yourself. If you have not studied the Word of God, it cannot dwell in you, and you will not have the tools you need to even pray or praise through difficult times. You can only experience the fullness of God's joy and love if you know "thus says the Lord."

Through all the prayer, praising, and studying of God's Word, you must also persevere. You must endure. Endurance produces character. Whenever I faced a difficult situation while growing up, my mother would tell me that God was producing character in me. When things got really rough, I respectfully told her that I didn't want any more character. In truth, I did want character, but I just didn't like the cost of it.

Counting the Cost of Character

The word *character* suggests that the person has been proven reliable. As we endure life challenges, as we persevere through rough times, the Lord is trying to make us into the kind of women God can depend on, the kind of women who will represent God well, the kind of women who can be used for God's glory. "My sisters, whenever you face trials of any kind, consider it nothing but joy, because you know that the testing of your faith produces endurance; and let endurance have its full effect, so that you may be mature and complete, lacking in nothing" (James 1:2-4).

"Suffering produces endurance, and endurance produces character, and character produces hope," Paul assures us, and Paul spoke from experience (Romans 5:3-4). Though it may seem impossible, the right attitude toward suffering and difficulty will yield positive results. Through it all, you will begin to have hope for the future.

Learning to Let Go

During this difficult time in my life, I grew to understand the pain I felt no longer had redemptive value. I had to let it go completely. There was nothing more for me to learn. You, too, have suffered long enough. You have learned the lessons. It's time to let it go. Whatever is holding you back, impeding your progress, weighing you down, keeping you from flying high and free, get rid of it.

"But how?" you ask. "I've been carrying it so long, I don't know how to let go." Well, Jesus provides this prescription:

> Jesus answered them, "Have faith in God. Truly I tell you, if you say to this mountain, 'Be taken up and thrown into the sea,' and if you do not doubt in your heart, but believe that what you say will come to pass, it will be done for you. So I tell you, whatever you ask for in prayer, believe that you have received it, and it will be yours." (Mark 11:22-24)

Mountain-moving faith is what allows you to let go. Mountain-moving faith in God is the source of power and authority by which we meet head-on the mountains, the difficulties, and the challenges in our lives. Mountain-moving faith is faith that believes and does not doubt.

"If you say to this mountain...," Jesus said. Mountain-moving faith literally speaks to mountains. Sounds ridiculous, doesn't it? But Jesus' words are true. You must speak to your mountain or, in other words, confess your faith.

Opening Both Mouth and Hands

The Hebrew word that English Bibles translate as "confess" is *yad*, meaning an open or extended hand. In Proverbs 18:21, *yad* is used in the context of power and means. "Death and life are in the power of the tongue, and those who love it will eat its fruits." In this verse, the tongue is depicted as having a hand that can literally grab or release something. The writer of Proverbs says that, with the tongue, we can grab hold of or release life or death. Put simply, the words we speak have power. They are like seeds that, when planted, develop into fruit-bearing plants. If we speak words of faith, we will bear the fruit of faith. On the other hand, if we speak doubt and fear, we will reap the fruit of doubt and fear.

When we confess the promises of God, take hold of the promises, stand on the promises, we can begin to see the fruit of the promises manifested in our lives. By confidently and consistently confessing our faith, we release the power of God's hand to work in our lives and on our situations. By faith, we can speak to difficult situations and command them to leave our lives. By faith, we can open our mouths in praise and open our hands in worship and service to accomplish the divine promises and plans our lips have already confessed.

This is no magical formula. I'm not talking about a "name it and claim it" religion. I'm talking about the power of the resources of prayer and praise that we have available to us. We must affirm that we know what God wants to see happen in our lives, believing that by the power of the Holy Spirit, it shall be done. After all, it is not until we affirm that belief that we will begin to act on it!

When I decided that it was time to be totally free of the grief of not being married and being in that relationship, I started speaking to my grief, "It's time for you to go. I can make it without you. My God shall supply all my needs according to his riches in Christ Jesus." Like the woman with the issue of blood, I reached out and touched Jesus' garment, knowing that by imagining a different reality for myself and then acting on that reality in faith, I could be made whole. Like that woman, I touched the hem of Jesus' garment knowing the power it holds to bring joy into my turbulent situation. Like her, by faith I was made whole, complete. I was released to fly.

My prayer is that you will become a woman who is able to fly above your turbulent circumstances. Through mountain-moving faith, reach out and touch Jesus. And you, too, will be made a whole woman, a woman with wings, a woman who loves to fly.

Shaped for Satisfaction

O God, you are my God, I seek you,
   my soul thirsts for you;
 my flesh faints for you,
   as in a dry and weary land where there is no water.
So I have looked upon you in the sanctuary,
   beholding your power and glory.
Because your steadfast love is better than life,
   my lips will praise you.
So I will bless you as long as I live;
   I will lift up my hands and call on your name.

My soul is satisfied as with a rich feast,
   and my mouth praises you with joyful lips
when I think of you on my bed,
   and meditate on you in the watches of the night;
for you have been my help,
   and in the shadow of your wings I sing for joy.
                              —Psalm 63:1-7

Decisions, Decisions, Decisions

Psalm 32:8; Isaiah 49:17

Life is a series of choices. From the very moment we open our eyes—if we decide to open our eyes—we choose whether or not to get out of bed. We choose whether to speak to the people we live with. We choose to take a bath, shower, birdbath, or just go out au naturel. We choose to have breakfast or go without, to go to work, to class, to the mall, or to stay in our rooms. Yes, life is a series of choices.

In addition to deciding among the mundane choices of daily living, we also face choices about how we are going to live. Every day we are faced with choices between right and wrong and good, better, and best. As Christians, a major choice that each of us makes is whether we will live up to who we have been created to be or be conformed to the way of the world.

How to Choose?

Everyone needs help in making good decisions. How does one choose a mate or a date? How do you decide whether to have sex before marriage? How do you decide, once you are married, whether to stay married when you realize that the one you married is not who or what you expected? What is your destiny? What is God's plan and purpose for your life? Perhaps your boss has offered you a promotion if you do things that are not in keeping with your values. You may have several options in terms of a career; which is the best one for you? You may have found that you are pregnant and are wondering whether to keep the baby. Maybe your baby's daddy doesn't want to get married, but he wants to live with you. What do you do?

Many of the choices that we have to make are not easy. I know from experience that it is not easy to be a young, gifted, and, perhaps, single woman in the world. You want to be happy; you want to be satisfied; you want to be fulfilled. You want what you want when you want it. The question you must always ask yourself when faced with life choices is whether what you want is what you need and deserve. Is it the best for you?

It is not always easy making the right choice. Although we Christians are no longer of the world, we are still in the world, some of us in more ways than we want to admit. We still think like the world thinks and still have worldly friends who influence our thoughts and behaviors. We still see things from a worldly viewpoint, because every day we get our share of a worldly perspective through television, radio, newspaper, and e-mail.

Appearances Deceive

We sometimes make choices based on the way something looks. If it looks good, it must be good. But things are not always as they appear. Everything that glitters ain't gold, and everything that looks good to you ain't necessarily good for you.

One day I was in a bank in downtown Atlanta when the best-looking man I think I have ever seen started walking toward me. I tried not to look too excited or too interested, even though I was. This brother was well-dressed from head to toe. His hair and mustache were neatly groomed, his fingernails clipped and buffed. His teeth sparkled, and he carried an expensive leather briefcase. Yet, as soon as he approached me and reached out his hand to introduce himself, his briefcase became unlatched and fell open. To my surprise, the briefcase was empty. This indicated to me that this brother was not all he appeared to be. I concluded that he was a fraud. He looked good, smelled nice, and walked like he was on his way somewhere, but I questioned whether he was going anywhere at all.

It is important that we consider the totality of the circumstances when we are making choices in life. We cannot judge anyone or anything without careful and thorough consideration. We can't make choices solely by the way something looks.

Feelings Can't Be Trusted

We sometimes base our choices on how something feels. The world says, "Do what you feel; go for what you want." The choices we have to make are often complicated because they involve matters of the heart. I have trouble making emotional decisions, especially when my passion gets involved. For years, I was largely governed by my feelings. If something felt right, then it must be right. However, I have come to understand that I cannot always trust my feelings. The Bible warns us, "The heart is devious above all else; it is perverse—who can understand it?" (Jeremiah 17:9).

Guidelines for Good Decision Making

If we cannot depend on what we see or what we feel in making choices, then what can we rely on? How do we make the right choices in life in the face of all the information constantly being thrown at us? How do we know what is right when many choices are not black and white? How do we make the right decisions when so many decisions are subjective? How do we garner the courage to do the right thing?

Whatever choices you face, keep these principles in mind to determine the best path for you:

- If a decision will require you to compromise who you are, your principles, and your values, then it is not the best thing for you.
- If a choice requires you to become less than who you are, to act as if you are not as intelligent, as organized, as insightful, and as wise as you are, then it is not the best thing for you.
- If a decision requires you to do all the giving or taking— that is; if there is no mutual exchange or relationship— then it is not in your best interest.

- If you are not at real peace about a decision, then it is not the best thing for you.

When I was younger and on my own for the first time, I knew that I needed to make my own decisions. Yet I did not feel equipped to do so. I often depended on the advice of friends. But after making some bad decisions even with their advice, I realized that I could not depend upon friends' advice when making life choices. That's when I turned to God. You see, God has certain expectations and desires for our lives. Yet, because God is gentle, God does not make us do anything. Instead, God has given us the ability to choose. While God doesn't force us to do anything, God doesn't leave us to make choices all by ourselves. Because God loves us and wants the best for us, God gives us the resources we need to make good choices. Those resources are contained in the Word of God.

God teaches us what is best for us through the Word! The Word of God is our first guide for all our decisions and choices. Scripture teaches, "All scripture is inspired by God and is useful for teaching, for reproof, for correction, and for training in righteousness, so that everyone who belongs to God may be proficient, equipped for every good work" (2 Timothy 3:16). God's Word is powerful! In it, we find precepts, principles, and promises that provide us with everything we need for godly living.

Precepts
Through biblical precepts, God gives us nonnegotiable commands and directives. In everyday life, a speed limit is an example of a precept. When a sign says that the speed limit is sixty-five miles per hour, then you are to drive sixty-five miles per hour. The Bible contains a number of precepts or nonnegotiable directives. They include:

- "This is my commandment, that you love one another as I have loved you" (John 15:12).
- "Forgive, and you will be forgiven; give, and it will be given to you" (Luke 6:37-38).

- "Do not be conformed to this world, but be transformed by the renewing of your minds" (Romans 12:2).

Principles

The Word of God also provides principles. These are general guidelines that require wisdom and discernment when applying them. An example from everyday life is a yellow caution light, which means "Proceed at your own risk." A few biblical examples include:

- "Therefore walk in the way of the good, and keep to the paths of the just" (Proverbs 2:20).
- "Whoever heeds instruction is on the path to life, but one who rejects a rebuke goes astray" (Proverbs 10:17).
- "'All things are lawful for me,' but not all things are beneficial. 'All things are lawful for me,' but I will not be dominated by anything" (1 Corinthians 6:12).

Promises

Finally, God makes promises on which we can build our futures, promises that assure us of God's love, presence, and provision. And Scripture itself testifies that God's promises are trustworthy. Numbers 23:19 declares "God is not a human being, that he should lie, or a mortal, that he should change his mind. Has he promised, and will he not do it? Has he spoken, and will he not fulfill it?" (Numbers 23:19).

Some biblical promises are unconditional; many others are connected to and contingent upon us keeping a precept or honoring a principle. Just a few of the hundreds of biblical promises include:

- "Trust in the LORD with all your heart, and do not rely on your own insight. In all your ways acknowledge him, and he will make straight your paths" (Proverbs 3:5-6).
- "I will put my law within them, and I will write it on their hearts; and I will be their God, and they shall be my people" (Jeremiah 31:33).

- "And remember, I am with you always, to the end of the age" (Matthew 28:20).
- "My God will fully satisfy every need of yours according to his riches glory in Christ Jesus" (Philippians 4:19).

Getting into God

Relying on God's precepts, principles, and promises to make the best choices for your life is essential for making good decisions. Making the right choices and decisions requires knowledge of God and of God's Word. You have to have more than a casual acquaintance with the Lord and with the Scriptures. As Psalm 119:11 advises, you must hide the Word of God in your heart.

To know the Word of God, we have to engage it daily. It is not enough to simply hear the Word on Sunday and get another dose at Bible study or midweek service. You must study the Word for yourself. Listening to tapes of sermons or teachings on the radio is helpful, but it is also important to read, study, and meditate on the Word during times of personal devotion. God's words lead us to know what is best for us.

God also instructs us through prayer. If you want to make the right choices in your life, pray and ask God what you should do. Sometimes God will give direct instructions. Other times, God will give us the wisdom to discern and understand what choices to make. Wisdom is the God-given ability to perceive the true nature of a matter and to implement the will of God in that matter. God grants wisdom to anyone who asks: "If any of you is lacking in wisdom, ask God, who gives to all generously and ungrudgingly, and it will be given to you" (James 1:5).

When I was younger, I thought people became wise with age, experience, or education. As a result, I assumed that I could not become wise at my age, with my lack of experience and education. I later discovered that I had taken a worldly perspective on wisdom.

Human wisdom and godly wisdom are quite different. God gives wisdom through discernment to those of us who desire it and then seek it. Receiving God's wisdom is nothing mystical or mysterious. The Holy Spirit gives the ability to discern what is real and true.

Facing Consequences with Courage

We are often fearful about making certain decisions, because those choices may have grave consequences. Such was the case with Shadrach, Meshach, and Abednego, whose story is told in the Old Testament book of Daniel. Shadrach, Meshach, and Abednego found themselves in quite a predicament. The king threatened to throw them into the fiery furnace if they didn't bow to him. Their story speaks so powerfully to us because it teaches us how to live courageously and to trust God, even when we do not know what the outcome will be.

Shadrach, Meshach, and Abednego were gifted young men. They had been taken from their native land and had been placed in the king's household. While there, they faced a series of choices. First, they were asked to compromise their convictions by eating the king's meat that had been offered to idols. Based on their upbringing in the Jewish faith, they chose not to eat the king's meat; instead, they ate only vegetables. God honored their faithfulness by making them ten times healthier than the other young men. Next, they were faced with the choice of bowing down to the king or burning in a fiery furnace. For most of us, an instance like this would cause our natural wisdom to kick in. We wouldn't want to burn, so it would be easier to bow.

- Having an abortion may seem to be best thing for everyone involved, but is it the right thing to do?
- Lying to keep others from being hurt may seem like the kindest thing, but is it really?
- Cheating on a test to keep your scholarship may seem like the only thing to do under the circumstances, but is it God's way?

God's wisdom says, take your stand. God commands you never to bow down to any idol. Trust God. If you lose your scholarship or have to drop out of school for a time, if your so-called friends cut you loose, if you lose your job or do not go out on another date for a while because you refused to bow down, it will be all right, I promise you. God will take care of you. Remember, "Trust in the LORD with all your heart and do not rely on your own insight" (Proverbs 3:5). That is what these three young men had to do. Shadrach, Meshach, and Abednego took a stand and left the consequences up to God. They believed that God would take care of them and knew what was best for them. They were willing to do what God said and not be afraid.

While some choices may be difficult to make in the moment, when we act in accordance with God's wisdom and God's will, the end result is worth any difficulty. There is a peace that comes from knowing that you have done the right thing. Those three Hebrew young men exercised their faith in God. God not only brought them out of the difficult situation, God made them a powerful witness to the king. You see, when you take a stand for what is right, you represent God in the world.

Of course, courage comes more easily when you don't stand alone. I thank God that we can also learn what is best for us through others who will give us godly counsel. There are lots of folk who give advice, but fewer who will give advice that is rooted in God and God's Word. I suggest that you surround yourself with people who have the same Christian values as you, people who have taken the same stand before you, who will stand beside you now, and who will help you keep standing in the future. You need people in your corner who love the Lord and desire to honor God with their whole beings. You need people who want to see you succeed, people who study the Word with you, people who will have your back when you're seeking God's face. Yes, get some godly counsel.

From Deciding It to Doing It

Now, sometimes we know what to do because we have sought God through the Word; we have prayed, sought godly counsel, and used our own discernment. We may have repeatedly received confirmation about what our decision needs to be. It's clear what we need to do. Yet we don't always follow through with our decisions. We may decide to do something, but we don't actually *do* the something we decide. That's where real courage comes in.

Knowing what is best for you is only half the battle; having the courage to do what is best can be more difficult! My advice? Seek and then use the power of the Holy Spirit. The Holy Spirit will give supernatural power and strength of will to do that which we cannot do on our own. Indeed, I join with Paul in saying, "I pray that, according to the riches of [God's] glory, he may grant that you may be *strengthened in your inner being with power through his Spirit*, and that Christ may dwell in your hearts through faith, as you are being rooted and grounded in love" (Ephesians 3:16-17, emphasis added).

Decisions, decisions, decisions. There are so many to make. Yet we are not powerless in making choices for our lives. God gives us powerful tools to help us. Stay connected to the Power Source, and you will live a life that is powerful beyond measure.

A Happier, Healthier You

1 Corinthians 6:19-20

About seven years ago, during a routine medical checkup, my doctor found that my blood pressure was elevated, and he recommended that I take medication to control it. Given my family history, I wasn't surprised by the diagnosis, but I was determined not to have to take medication for the rest of my life.

So I told the doctor to give me thirty days to get my blood pressure controlled through natural means. I immediately began a daily walking regimen. Every morning, I got up, put on my sneakers, and stepped out onto the streets of my neighborhood. At first, I strolled, but then I worked up to an intense power walk. I started out taking level streets with no hills and then progressed to climbing the hills to get my heart rate higher. I could feel the strengthening in my legs and buttocks and actually enjoyed the benefits walking provided. Every step I took, I believed, helped lower my blood pressure and elevate my metabolism. I was burning calories and losing weight in addition to firming my thighs, stomach, and hips. Thirty days later, when I went back to the doctor, he was amazed, and so was I. My blood pressure had lowered significantly.

In addition to physical benefits, walking also helped me spiritually. I was accustomed to an early morning rendezvous with God at home, so when I started walking early in the morning, I talked to God. My physical activity developed into a spiritual activity. Like the psalmist, I can attest, "O LORD, in the morning you hear my voice; in the morning I plead my case to you, and watch" (Psalm 5:3).

I spent each morning walking and talking with God, getting my mind, soul, and body in shape. Walking did wonders for my attitude, because, while walking, I prepared myself for the challenges of the day. My spirit soared as I walked. I was happy and relaxed and felt I could take on the world when I finished. And I did.

As I have continued to exercise and shape up this body, I have become happier and healthier. I have also discovered the importance of keeping my body in shape as an act of worship. You may be wondering why keeping your body in shape is worthy of discussion outside of a health class or a doctor's office. Many of us only begin taking care of our bodies after the doctor tells us to do so. If my doctor had not threatened to put me on medication for high blood pressure, I may never have made exercise a part of my daily life. But as I began to reap the physical and spiritual benefits of exercising, I began to recognize that my body is not just a body; it is the temple of the living God. Paul makes this fact clear: "Or do you not know that your body is a temple of the Holy Spirit within you, which you have from God, and that you are not your own? For you were bought with a price; therefore glorify God in your body" (1 Corinthians 6:19-20).

Maintaining God's Temple

Our bodies are where the Holy Spirit dwells. God can't live in a body that is in just any kind of condition. Think about what kind of house you live in or would like to live in. You wouldn't be comfortable with a run-down dwelling. You would prefer one that is in good condition and beautiful to behold on the inside and out.

Keeping the temple in shape is about feeling good and looking good. Like it or not, looks matter. A woman ought to be sugar sharp every time she steps out! Everyone who sees her ought to ask, "Wow! Who is that lady?" I walked in the grocery store one day, and a young cashier told me how beautiful I looked, and he asked me out to dinner. Another man, who saw me in the airport, commented that I must have taken good care

of myself when I was younger. I told him, "I did, and I still do."
Be clear that God wants you, the temple in which God dwells,
to be beautiful, inside and out. After all, you are a person of
worth and value, and that ought to show on the inside as well
as on the outside.

Our entire lives, including our bodies, are a gift from God.
God expects us to take good care of ourselves! Therefore, we
have to adopt healthy eating, exercise, and other good habits as
a part of our lifestyles.

From Good Food to Better Eating

After I committed myself to exercising, I still wasn't eating right,
even after my personal trainer encouraged me to do so. Truth
be told, I didn't want to eat right. I loved the way that I was
eating. I ate anything and everything I wanted, whenever and
however I wanted. I had not given up any food except pork and
beef, which I had eliminated from my diet years ago. My favorite
foods included soda, chocolate cake, potato chips, and french
fries. Moreover, I loved to eat late at night. Well, you can imagine
that, with these eating habits, I was a little overweight. Though
tall and stately, I had a behind you could set a dish on.

Nevertheless, I vehemently fought my trainer about eating
better. I didn't think what I ate made a difference. I had a similar
attitude about eating that the church at Corinth did about doing
to their bodies what they wanted. That is why Paul had to remind
them that their bodies belonged to God. Not only did God create
their bodies, but God had paid a high price for them. The least
they could do in return was to honor God with their bodies.
Honoring God by keeping God's temple healthy is the least we
can do, as well.

How do we do it? Paul's letter to the Corinthian church
provides us with further instructions. In 1 Corinthians 6:12,
Paul says: "All things are lawful for me, but not all things are
beneficial." Ask yourself if what you are eating is really beneficial
for you. Will it enhance or hurt you physically? Many of us feel
the sweeter or more fattening a food is, the better it tastes. We

also feel that we should eat as much of any item we want. While there is nothing in Scripture that forbids us from eating whatever we want, Scripture does forbid gluttony or overindulging in ways that are harmful to us. Foods with high sodium content may lead to high blood pressure. A high-fat, high-cholesterol diet may lead to diabetes, obesity, heart disease, stroke, and a myriad of other life-threatening illnesses. Eating whatever you want may be permissible, but you must ask yourself, is it beneficial?

I contemplated all the benefits of healthy eating, but I was still unconvinced. Ultimately, my decision to eat better began with a vision. One Sunday I saw a young woman who was tall and slender and had every hair in place sitting in the congregation. She looked like I used to look the year I graduated from high school. Vanity kicked in. If I was going to look like that again, I knew that exercise was not enough and that I needed to change my eating habits. I was finally ready.

To sustain healthy eating habits, we must first understand the purpose of food as well as our relationship to food. The purpose of food is to provide the energy the body needs to sustain itself. However, most of us do not limit food to its primary purpose. In fact, many of us do not even think of food as energy at all.

Enjoyment without Excess

For most of us, food is also true pleasure. We hardly, if ever, eat solely for nourishment; we eat because we love to eat. Some of us get great joy in thinking about what we are going to eat, morning, noon, and night. When my sister was a child, she would wake up in the morning asking, "What's for breakfast?" When she finished breakfast, she would ask, "What's for lunch?" And as soon as she finished lunch, she would ask, "What's for dinner?" The only thing my sister seemed to think about was eating. If we are honest, food is all some of us think about, too.

Food should be an enjoyable experience. Eating is a social event, especially for us Christians. We love to have potluck dinners, meetings around meals, receptions, and teas after every affair. With our families and friends, we gather around the table and outside on the deck for traditional meals. It is good to enjoy food, as long as we don't use it in excess and eat for reasons other than nutrition and enjoyment.

Unfortunately, while some people wrestle with addictions to drugs, booze, tobacco, or even work, for others of us, food is our drug of choice. We use it to cope with stress, pain, unhappiness, and loneliness. Whenever we feel unloved, we take refuge in food. We use food to handle bad news or to bury our problems. Sometimes our eating habits become symptomatic of deeply rooted emotional problems. When we think we are undesirable, we will eat and gain weight out of a sense of despair or in search of comfort. Sometimes women who were sexually molested (especially as children) will intentionally gain weight to create an unattractive wall around themselves. (Some women have a very different relationship with food. Eating disorders such as anorexia and bulimia starve us of nourishment in an attempt to lose pounds that aren't "extra" at all or as a way of reasserting control over bodies that have been vulnerable or over lives that seem chaotic.)

Food is neither the source of nor the answer to our problems. Like any other drug, when we come down off the high that food gives us, the problem is still there, and there are side effects like being overweight.

We have to become aware of what our issues are, and we must deal with them in healthier and more effective ways, through prayer and with counseling. Whether we struggle with issues that are caused by things done to us or with those issues that are all a part of life and living, we can decide whether those struggles will make us bitter or better. Each of us must learn to love, accept, and care for ourselves, even when we believe that no one else does. God cares and wants the best for us!

Eating a well-balanced diet is key to optimum health. There are hosts of eating plans developed by experts that can assist you if you need guidance. If you need one-on-one assistance, seek the advice of a nutritionist. Whatever you choose, make sure it is a plan that you can stick with for life. Some fad diets provide quick results but are difficult to sustain. Whatever extra weight you are carrying did not come on overnight, and it won't come off overnight, either.

Healthy Habits for a Happy You

Cultivate other habits to become a happy, healthier you. Earlier, I mentioned exercise. I chose walking, but I encourage you to choose a form of regular physical activity that you enjoy and can commit to doing nearly every day of the week. If it's dancing, dance! If it's running, run! If it's gardening, plant! But by all means, move God's temple. You will look good and feel good, too.

Having regular medical checkups is also essential. Pap smears, mammograms, blood pressure checks, and diabetes screenings are vital to maintaining good health. Doctors recommend various tests at certain stages in life. Get your physician's advice about what tests you may need, given your age, physical condition, and family history.

Pampering yourself is also key to becoming a happier and healthier you. Getting your hair done and enjoying periodic manicures, pedicures, massages, or facials are wonderful ways to pamper yourself. Taking bubble baths, layering fragrances, and wearing matching underwear can make you feel and look good. When you look good, you tend to feel better.

Getting proper rest is also vital to healthy living. As women, we tend to burn the candle at both ends. We are everybody's everything—at home, on the job, and at church. If you are going to be any good to anybody, including yourself, you must be well rested. Experts say that adults need an average of seven to eight hours of sleep every night. How many hours did you get last night?

Finally, whether you are young or mature, able-bodied or not so able-bodied, healthy or suffer with chronic disease, live the life that you have been given to the fullest. Jesus came that you might have life and that more abundantly. The choice is yours to live the life that Jesus promised. The choice is yours to take care of the temple in which God's Spirit has elected to live. Choose health. Choose joy. Choose life.

Single Satisfaction

Philippians 3:10-13

In case you are wondering whether I am qualified to address the issue of singlehood, know that I am an expert in the field. I am not someone who had to read up on the subject and is now married and has to remember what it was like. You see, I live the single life every single day. In fact, I've known nothing else. At fifty-six years of age, I've never been married. I have never even had anyone ask me to marry him, at least not seriously. I know some of you who have seen me before are thinking that anyone as beautiful and intelligent as I am ought to have a husband by now. So, what's up with that?

Believe me, you are not the first to ask that question. In fact, some of you have been asked the very same questions. "What's a sweet thing like you doing single?" "Why hasn't someone scooped you up?" "You're quite a catch; so, why haven't you been caught?"

Concerned family, friends, and others ask, "What are you waiting for? We were hoping to live to see you married with children." Or "I was counting on you for grandchildren." Like you, I don't have the answers to their questions. Like you, I don't know why I'm still single.

I have struggled with being single for many years, agonizing over the fact that I have not been chosen. I have felt rejected and have wondered what in the world is wrong with me. You may be wondering the same things about yourself and, at times, may have felt unwanted and undesirable.

Even though we may not have the answers, our family and friends seem to have no problem solving the mystery of our singleness. They say we're too smart, too tall, too short, that we make too much money or not enough, that we're too bossy, too passive, too controlling, too shy, too aggressive, too neat, too messy, too moody, too fat, too thin, too mean, too crazy, and—my personal favorite—too intimidating!

Others accuse us of being way too particular. It is true that some of us have lists of the qualities we want in a mate that no human could possibly fulfill. Still, we cannot settle for less than God's best for us. Perhaps we've tried settling, only to be sorely disappointed. Those brothers may have been good men, just not the right ones for us.

Self-Esteem and Singleness

The more people try to explain why we are single, the more we begin to believe that we are somehow flawed. Even those of us who have developed a level of comfort with our singleness may begin to wonder if there is something wrong with us that explains why no one has claimed us. We begin to say to ourselves, "If only I were [you fill in the blank], then I would be married."

These feelings of inadequacy affect our self-esteem. Too many of us struggle with low self-esteem anyway, and the fact that we are not married causes our self-esteem to plummet even lower. We even question why God made us the way he made us. However, God asks us through the apostle Paul, "But who indeed are you, a human being, to argue with God? Will what is molded say to the one who molds it, 'Why have you made me like this?' Has the potter no right over the clay, to make out of the same lump one object for special use and another for ordinary use?" (Romans 9:20-21).

You are who you are because God made you that way. You are a marvelous work. Though there are some things about you that need molding, there are plenty of women who are just as aggressive, moody, bossy, sassy, mean, or crazy as you are who are happily married. Our singleness is a mystery. It is not that something is wrong with us. We are not perfect beings, but we cannot allow our imperfections to cause us to doubt our worth.

God is not punishing us for being who we were created to be, nor is God punishing us for things we have done in the past. Perhaps there are things about your past that you are not too proud of, like having been sexually active outside of marriage. We've all done things we are not proud of, even married folk. But God is a forgiving God. God loves us and blesses us in spite of our shortcomings and mistakes. The opportunities that we lost because of our disobedience may no longer be available to us, but God gives us another chance.

Whatever the reason, singleness is our reality, at least for now. I used to talk about singleness as being a season, but for me and perhaps for you, too, that season has become a lifetime, or at least it seems that way. I cannot change the fact that I am single, but I can decide how I'm going to deal with it. Those of us who are single and want to marry have to first work through and express our negative feelings about being single. Acknowledging our desire to marry is not bad in and of itself, unless the desire is rooted in a feeling of inadequacy because we are single. We also need to separate our own negative feelings from those that have been imposed on us by others. We have to stop worrying about what other people think about us because we are not married. Do not allow the judgment of others to influence your choices or to make you feel inadequate about the choices you have made.

We must also commit ourselves to always being our true selves. In romantic relationships, too many of us tend to become whatever we think the other person wants us to be. The changes may be superficial: We may lose weight, dress more conservatively, or let our hair grow. Other alterations are more fundamental: We may become less assertive, more mild-mannered, and constrain our "oversized" personalities so that he won't be intimidated. These changes go beyond the typical give-and-take of any enduring relationship; the changes are not motivated by a healthy spirit of compromise in which both parties give ground to meet somewhere in the middle. No, too many of us remake ourselves in the image of a man's ideal woman—and we lose our true selves in the process.

If there are things that need to be changed in your life, change them for you and for your God, not for someone else. But know that the core of who God made you is unchangeable. Whoever you find yourself in relationship with needs to love you for who you are at that very moment and not for who he wants you to be or who you may become.

Satisfaction and Singleness

If you think that living the single life is challenging today, consider how much more difficult it must have been during the apostle Paul's day, when marriage was considered the only legitimate lifestyle, especially for women. Yet Paul, writing his first letter to the church at Corinth, affirms the value of singleness in the family of God.

Paul even went so far as to offer this principle (but not a precept) for the believer who found herself single: "In my judgment she is more blessed if she remains as she is. And I think that I too have the Spirit of God" (1 Corinthians 7:40). He goes on to describe singleness as a calling for those who have the gift of celibacy. (I know you are hoping not to be so gifted!) Although Paul affirms marriage, he puts singleness on par with marriage. In fact, he said that he wished all persons were like he was—single and satisfied to be so!

Some women have discovered the blessing that Paul talked about and choose to remain single in order to pursue vocational and other personal endeavors. Such women enjoy the freedom of single life—freedom to come and go, to choose for ourselves, to consider only God's will and no one else's in our lives. It seems that this freedom was of value to Jesus as well, who by all accounts remained single in the Jewish culture where *all* men married. If it was good enough for Jesus…! To choose to remain a strong, satisfied single woman is a legitimate choice, no matter what the culture (or church) may say.

Unfortunately, far too many of us feel incomplete as single persons. Like Jesus and Paul, we are a part of a society that lifts up marriage and family life as the way to be happy and whole.

If a woman is not married, she is thought to be incomplete and living an unfulfilled life. We have been led to believe that we lack something because we don't have a mate. So we are always looking for our "better half," or we have placed our lives on hold waiting for the "one."

When I was buying my first home, my mother felt that I should just continue to live in an apartment, because she believed that if I acquired too many things, a man would feel as if he was not needed. I believe that if we spend our lives waiting on someone to come along and complete us, we will miss out on all the joys and blessings that God has for us right now. We dare not place our lives on hold. Nor should we believe that we are incomplete. Our completeness and sufficiency come from Christ. We are as complete as we are ever going to be through Jesus: "For in him the whole fullness of deity dwells bodily, and you have come to fullness in him, who is the head of every ruler and authority" (Colossians 2:9-10).

As sisters shaped in God's own image, no matter what our relationship status may be, we need to find satisfaction in becoming the piece of work God plans for us to be! And step one is refusing to think of any future spouse as that "other (or better) half." When God promised Adam a helper, God was promising him someone who would complement him. The two would come together like a hand and glove—not like two halves that make a whole.

When we go into a marriage, we need to be whole already. If you go into a marriage expecting the other person to *complete* you rather than *complement* you, then you are putting an unnecessary strain on the relationship and the other person. God made you complete in yourself. When the Lord said it wasn't good for Adam to be alone, God was only observing his human need for companionship—someone to enhance his life, not to make his life complete. The same is true for you and for me. Our wholeness is found not in another human being, no matter how fine or strong or skilled or tender he may be. Wholeness is found only in the God who created us in the divine image.

Solitude and Singleness

Even those of us who have embraced our singleness and who find our completeness in Christ still face challenges as we go through life solo. Loneliness is one of those challenges.

Some singles not only struggle with being alone, some of us downright hate it. We go to work alone, eat out alone, and go to church alone. We can't stand being home alone, so we play the television and the stereo at the same time. We constantly talk on the phone as a way of keeping company. But being *alone* does not have to mean being *lonely*.

Loneliness is not caused by our singleness. There are plenty of married people who are lonely. Loneliness is actually a result of our humanness, of the fall of humans and resulting separation from God. When Adam and Eve sinned in the garden, they ruined their perfect union with God and one another. This act caused them to be estranged from God and one another, which resulted in their loneliness.

Loneliness is an attitude, a state of mind. You can be lonely in a crowd. Loneliness is a decision. When we are lonely, it may mean that we have not yet learned how to enjoy our own company. We have not yet realized the gift of being alone. Everyone needs time to be alone.

Think of it this way: Spending time alone is an investment. It is a time to recharge our emotional and spiritual batteries, to think and pray, to gain insight or a solution to a pressing problem. It is a time to rest after a battle, to find grace to deal with life. It's a time to hear from God.

Jesus looked for opportunities to be alone. As a matter of fact, he often withdrew from the crowds to a solitary place to pray. We all need time alone with ourselves and with God. Psalm 46:10 instructs us, "Be still, and know that I am God!" When we are alone and still, God is able to renew God's image in us. We need moments of aloneness to reflect, meditate, think, hear, and re-create ourselves by reconnecting with our Creator.

Sex and Singleness

Sexuality is another challenge that singles, particularly Christian singles, face. We are sexual beings. Before we became saved and realized that we are called to live a celibate life, many of us engaged in sex without much thought. Only now are we coming to an understanding of what it means to live holy. But celibacy isn't easy, especially when you have already been sexually active.

In 1 Corinthians 6:13-20, Scripture tells us that we are to flee from sexual immorality because our bodies are the temples of the Holy Spirit, whom we have received from God. We are not our own; we have been bought with a price; therefore, we are to honor God with our bodies.

Celibacy is a major challenge for many of us. Some of us, perhaps, wonder if God seriously expects this of us. We ask God incredulously, "Do you know what you are asking of me? After all, you were the one who created this powerful desire in me! It was you who gave me the ability to love and engage in the beautiful and powerful act of expressing love to and for another through sexual intimacy!"

Lately I've even found myself saying to God, "I know that you meant for me to live a celibate life at sixteen, twenty-six, and thirty-six years of age, but now that I'm fifty-six, there has to be a special concession, a special dispensation even!" After all, with age come wisdom, maturity, and responsibility. God couldn't possibly mean for me to live this way forever.

Here is the crux of the matter, however. God wisely gave us sexual intimacy as a way of consummating a covenant relationship and becoming one with another in marriage. Therefore, God intends for us to be fully committed to the person we become one with sexually. God didn't intend for us to become one with just anybody and everybody. Some of us may believe that we can't say no. But with God's help, we can. I'm living proof. "For the grace of God has appeared, bringing salvation to all, training us to renounce impiety and worldly passions, and in the present age to live lives that are self-controlled, upright, and godly" (Titus 2:11-12).

Make Up Your Mind

I have discovered some important things about living a celibate lifestyle. First, you have to make up your mind to be celibate. Sexual abstinence while unmarried, after a divorce, or after the death of a mate requires a conscious decision and act of the will. Living a celibate lifestyle requires planning. Ask yourself, "How am I going to handle a dinner date with a fine man? How am I going to respond if he asks me back to his house?" If you fail to plan, you plan to fail.

Clean Up Your Thoughts

You have to clean up your thought life. Lust begins with a look. You see someone who turns you on, and you can't take your eyes off him. He sees you, your eyes meet, and there is instant chemistry. Your look turns from admiration to speculation and imagination, trying to figure out what it would be like to be in intimate sexual contact with that person.

Lust is causing you to fantasize and to feed the sexual urges and desires, and those thoughts can easily turn into sexual immorality. James 1:14-15 says, "But one is tempted by one's own desire, being lured and enticed by it; then, when that desire has conceived, it gives birth to sin, and that sin, when it is fully grown, gives birth to death."

Know Your Weaknesses

Know the areas where you are weak, where you are vulnerable, where you are most susceptible to temptation. Know what situations you can handle and those you can't. Take baby steps. We do not work out our weaknesses in sweeping, grand ways, but by taking baby steps every day. Scriptures such as this one guide us in the way:

> For this is the will of God, your sanctification: that you abstain from fornication; that each one of you know how to control your own body in holiness and honor, not with lustful passion, like the Gentiles who do not know God. . . . For God did not call us to impurity but in holiness. Therefore whoever rejects this rejects not human authority but God, who also gives his Holy Spirit to you. (1 Thessalonians 4:3-5,7-8)

Accept No Substitutes

Finally, we must recognize that sexual intercourse is no substitute for true intimacy. Most single adults are more intimacy starved than sexually deprived, as evidenced by the fact that we share the sheets with a man's body but not his soul. Intimacy requires us to enter another's space emotionally. Intimacy is believing in another person and having them believe in you. Intimacy is giving oneself to another, listening, loving, and caring for that person in good times and bad. Intimacy doesn't happen overnight. It takes time and involves risk and sacrifice. Intimacy requires vulnerability and trust. Sexual intimacy is no replacement for emotional intimacy. As difficult as it may be, we must honor God with our whole beings, from head to toe.

Contentment Despite Challenges

Yes, singleness has its challenges, and there are some things we should not do. There are also some positive choices you can and *should* make during this season. First and foremost, you can choose to be content. You see, whether you are single or married, God wants you to have life and that more abundantly. In all that Paul went through, persecution, imprisonment, even singleness, he learned, as he told the church at Philippi, to be content (see Philippians 4:11-13). He learned and committed himself to being victorious in spite of his circumstances. He did not need to have things his way, because he had found contentment in the rich, spiritual, and satisfying resources provided by Christ.

The English word *content* comes from a Latin root meaning "contained." It is a description of the woman whose resources are within so that she doesn't have to depend on external substitutes. When I am saved, Christ lives within, giving me everything I need for life and living. Christ offers the same riches to you.

Whether single or married, we can't look to another person to give us the security and satisfaction that we long for in life. We are created complete, yes, but no individual is sufficient in herself or in anyone else. Christ alone is our sufficiency. In him, we are restored to our created wholeness. In Christ, we learn contentment. We can do all things through Christ who gives us strength. Christ must be our single satisfaction.

I don't know how long your season of singleness (or mine, for that matter) will last, but I do know how to be satisfied and to make the most of the season. Get in touch with yourself. Grow, be stretched, and take advantage of experiences that will help you become all you need to be. Make good choices during this season of your life. Enjoy life while living holy. Be devoted totally to God. Make God your single satisfaction. You may not have chosen to be single, but you can choose to be satisfied with yourself. Live for today! Trust God to take care of tomorrow.

That's What Friends Are For

Ecclesiastes 4:9-12

Who among us has not already discovered that life can be a trip, especially for women? We contend with so much. We are expected to be all things to all people—loving wife and mother, supportive sister and friend, doting daughter and niece. We are expected to handle everyone else's affairs as well as our own.

Add to that the fact that most of us work full-time jobs. At times, the workplace is not a pleasant environment; supervisors, colleagues, and employees can make the workplace difficult at best or unbearable at worst. These difficult on-the-job personalities can make the reports, proposals, and projects that are always due seem insurmountable. Not to mention the fact that we are rarely, if ever, paid what we are worth.

Dealing with others might be more manageable if we didn't have our own personal issues pressing on us. Despite all the people around us, some of us are still lonely. Perhaps there are people in our lives but no significant other. Some of us may have no one to come home to, no one to hold us tight, no one to kiss goodnight. Some of us may be married, with or without children, and still be lonely. When you are in a relationship that is devoid of mutual love and respect and where communication is almost nonexistent, loneliness seems inevitable.

Health issues may also plague us, physically and emotionally. An abnormal pap smear or mass on a mammogram evokes terror. A miscarriage or tubal pregnancy may threaten our dreams of having children. Cervical cancer, lupus, heart disease, or other ailments may wrack our bodies. Broken hearts caused by people who have misused and abused us, disappointed and confused us, neglected or rejected us may leave us with emotional scars more devastating than physical ones.

After we got saved, we expected life to be abundant. We keep being told that we are more than conquerors. And yet we battle daily just to live right. Sometimes we succeed; sometimes we outright fail. Sometimes we are caught off guard by Satan, who presents us with opportunities that look good on the surface but that are designed to cause us to fall short of God's glory and to live lives of shame and condemnation.

A Little Help from a Friend

With all that we have to attend to, we wonder at times how we can not only survive this life, but also thrive. How can we manage the stresses and burdens? The answer to these questions lies in our understanding that if we are to manage this life, we cannot do it alone. I can testify that no matter how difficult the day or how emotionally or physically taxing the week, life is made livable, even enjoyable, with a little help from my friends.

Just knowing that someone who loves me and will listen to my issues without complaining, someone who will question my motives and make sure that I am not headed down a destructive path is just a phone call away makes all of life's messes and madness easier to bear.

The Teacher in Ecclesiastes expressed this very sentiment in the Old Testament:

> Two are better than one, because they have a good reward for their toil. For if they fall, one will lift up the other; but woe to one who is alone and falls and does not have another to help. Again, if two lie together, they keep warm; but how can one keep warm alone? And though one might prevail against another, two will withstand one. A threefold cord is not quickly broken. (4:9-12)

Despite being as wise and wealthy as he was, the author of Ecclesiastes realized that life was not intended to be lived independently. God created us as spiritual beings, first for relationship with God's self and then for relationships with one another. Women in particular seem emotionally constructed to desire someone with whom to walk through life. We need a good girlfriend to share our joys and our sorrows, to celebrate our triumphs, to bring warmth to our sometimes cold and bitter realities, and to watch our backs.

Girlfriends, sister-girls, and soul mates help us move through life, conquering fears and insecurities, helping us hold our heads up high when we have experienced defeat. Girlfriends will even keep us from hurting ourselves or someone else. Girlfriends have preserved the lives of innumerable husbands and boyfriends, children, crazy supervisors and supervisees, even challenging church members. Had it not been for the listening ear of my sister-friend the Reverend Dr. Margaret Elaine Flake, I would not have gotten through my most difficult times as a pastor. (Indeed, there are members of my church who don't realize that they owe their lives to her!) Yes, friends are lifesavers! They save your life and the lives of everyone else who pushes you to the limit.

Throughout this passage in Ecclesiastes, the Teacher makes clear the benefits of mutual friendship, friendships in which both people are full participants in the giving and taking and where there is shared responsibility for one another. No one wants to be in a one-sided relationship with anyone, especially not a sister-friend. We women tend to find ourselves as the primary givers and nurturers of too many relationships already. We need at least one relationship where the other meets us halfway, that allows us to be who we are with a person who is willing to work as hard in the relationship as we are. We each need at least one friend who will share her heart even as we share ours, who will be transparent, vulnerable, and available.

Of course, there will be times when one friend's needs are greater than the other's and when one friend carries the other through a difficult time. Yet when the other experiences a similar need, the comforted must become the comforter. It has to be a give-and-take thing. The Teacher is right. Two are better than one. Not only when it comes to friendship, but also when it comes to work. You and I both know that two working together cooperatively can accomplish more than one working independently. But let me tell you that when two sharp, capable, and awesome sisters unite their talents, skills, and abilities to work toward a common goal, the results are incredible. What happens in that exchange is what the writer of Proverbs was talking about: "Iron sharpens iron, and one [woman] sharpens the wits of another" (Proverbs 27:17).

Two women working together, sharing dreams, bouncing creative ideas off one another to develop plans and programs are an unbeatable combination. Having girlfriends who push us to excel, whose giftedness challenges us to work harder, whose ideas stretch us and will not allow us to be satisfied with the status quo or to settle for less than the best is a blessing.

At a time when I had the opportunity to either be satisfied with where I was as a pastor of a new church or to test the limits, God brought Margaret Elaine Flake into my life. She invited me to preach at Allen Cathedral AME Church in Queens, New York, to do workshops at their women's retreat. This was the first major women's retreat in which I had been invited to participate. My sister and friend had brought together more than twelve hundred women for the event. At that moment, I saw for the first time what was possible under a woman's leadership.

Dr. Flake is a master administrator with a phenomenal mind. She is creative and innovative. When it comes to iron sharpening iron, she is one sharp sister! Spending time with her allowed me to share hopes and dreams and stretched and shaped me for the next level of my ministry. When I returned home after our first encounter, I could not be satisfied with what I had achieved, because I knew God had so much more in store, and I intended to claim it. In the company of Dr. Flake and other women to whom she has introduced me over the years, I have become razor sharp, too!

That's what friends are for. We all need these kinds of friends in our lives—friends who are accomplishing something with their lives and with whom we can partner to be the best we can be. We need friends who bring out the best in us, who build us up instead of tearing us down.

Some of our friends are nice people, but not the best people for us. We are unequally yoked with some of our friends. Some of your friends may have abilities but no ambition. They may have a purpose but no plan. They may have ideas but no initiative; they may have gifts but no goals. Some of them are going nowhere in life. Some of them don't even want to go anywhere. They are satisfied with doing as little as possible with their lives. You cannot afford to hang with them. They are hindering your progress and holding you down. God has great plans for your life, as the prophet Jeremiah says, plans to prosper you and not to harm you, plans to give you hope and a future. You cannot afford to hang with anyone who cannot sharpen, empower, release, and help you go to the next level. Life is too precious. Life is too short for us to waste time fooling around with people who are unwilling to work to achieve their best.

Yes, two are better than one when you have a sister-friend who can work cooperatively with you to complete you and not compete with you. Two are also better than one when it comes to walking through life's challenges. If one falls down, her friend can help her up. But pity the woman who falls and has no one to help her up!

Friends Who Help You Up

During Old Testament times, roads and paths were not usually paved or leveled. Often, rocks hidden in the earth made travel dangerous. It was easy to slip and fall. It was not abnormal for even the most experienced traveler to stumble, perhaps breaking a limb or falling into a hidden pit.

Life is like that, too. There are all kinds of crooks and curves in the road. One has to be careful not to stumble and fall, both physically and spiritually. In our walk with the Lord, though we may intend to do what is right, there are always slippery places. There are opportunities presented to us that, if taken, will compromise our integrity, causing us to fall short of God's glory.

Sin can be so attractive that we suddenly find ourselves in its horrible grip, denying its reality, pretending and rationalizing that what we are doing is right. We think to ourselves, "Everyone else is doing it; I'm not hurting anyone." But Paul admonishes us, "[Sisters], if anyone is detected in a transgression, you who have received the Spirit should restore [her] in a spirit of gentleness. Take care that you yourselves are not tempted. Bear one another's burdens, and in this way you will fulfill the law of Christ" (Galatians 6:1-2).

Because we are all recovering from something, every one of us needs a girlfriend who will confront us when we are wrong and will help us walk upright. We have not always been saved. We have not always wanted to live right. Truth be told, some days we aren't all that sure we want to live right now. Living holy is hard work!

Friends Who Hold You Up

You need a spiritual girlfriend if you intend to live right. A spiritual girlfriend is one who is led by the fruit of the Spirit. When you fall, she needs to be able to confront you, speaking the truth in love without judging or condemning you. Once she picks you up from your fall, she needs to hold you accountable so that you don't make that same mistake again.

Most of us are repeat offenders. We don't do anything new; we just keep on committing the same offenses. We all have those cracks in our armor that Satan tries to use to bring us down. As a single woman who has made a commitment to be celibate, I have to be careful about my encounters with men. Even after more than twenty years (or perhaps *especially* after twenty years) and even with God's love constraining me to do what I know is right, this is an area of my life where Satan could trip me up. I know it because it has happened before. That's why I have a friend who keeps me accountable in that area of my life. Periodically, Claudette Copeland asks me how I'm doing and if I am standing strong. I know what she means. She wants to know if there is a strong temptation in my life. I always tell her the truth, and she helps talk me through my struggles.

Our girlfriends ought to be persons with whom we can share our deepest struggles, those with whom we can be honest. I have found that when I am able to expose to the light the sins, thoughts, and indiscretions over which I continue to stumble, those temptations lose their power over me. They no longer have the control they once had. The fear of being exposed is gone. The shame, condemnation, and guilt are taken away by a loving sister-friend who forgives and helps restore me. You ought to have such a sister-friend in your life!

Friends Who Patch You Up

If I fall, I know I can rely on Claudette and Elaine to restore me gently. In *Merriam-Webster's Medical Dictionary*, *restore* means "to bring back to or put back into a former or original state." In medicine, one may restore the alignment of a broken bone, restore feeling to a deadened nerve, or even restore life through cardio-pulmonary resuscitation. The process of physical restoration is nearly always painful, and it requires gentle hands and skillful touch.

Spiritual restoration is much the same. When we have fallen, we don't need someone to lecture or condemn us. We don't need anyone to tell us how disappointed God is with us or that we should be disappointed in ourselves. Rather, we need someone to be gentle with us. We need someone who knows that if it had not been for God's grace, she would have gotten caught up in the same stuff. We all need someone to accept us unconditionally as God has accepted us, and yet who holds us accountable and restores us to right relationship with God.

In the Galatians 6 passage, Paul says that we are to carry one another's burdens. When Paul talks about burdens, he is referring to those things we cannot carry by ourselves. Many of us are overburdened with things from our past or our present that simply need to be dumped or shared with someone. Sharing our burdens with others is liberating. If your friend is overburdened, lighten her load by giving her the gifts of your arms to hold her, your shoulder to lean on, and your heart to listen to her.

Friends Who Warm You Up

Two are better than one when it comes to keeping warm. In a world that is often cold and uncaring, we need support and encouragement from our friends. When is the last time you encouraged your friend by sending her a note telling her how special she is? How often do you affirm your sister-friend for who she is and what she has accomplished and is accomplishing in life? All of us need encouragement. Encouragement builds us up and gives us the confidence to be all that God created and gifted us to be. The story is told of a Realtor who was going through a really difficult time in her career. Because sales were down, she kept threatening to give up. Her sales manager, who was also a good friend, kept reminding her daily of her abilities and her past successes. Today that frustrated Realtor is a million-dollar seller, one of the top real estate agents in the business, all because her friend believed in her.

We need encouragement when we are going through difficult times. But we also need to know that someone has our back. Although one may be overpowered, two can defend themselves. A cord of three strands is not quickly broken. Dangers confront us every day of our lives. There are people who seek to do us harm. We encounter envious people who don't want to see us succeed. (Know that they are not the real enemy; they are simply a vehicle for Satan to kill, steal, and destroy.)

By ourselves, we can easily be overpowered, but with a little help from our friends, we can defend ourselves. With prayer, we create a cord of three strands that is not easily broken. Praying with and for our friends is both powerful and effective. I invite you, if don't already, to begin to pray with and for your friends. Take her concerns to God in prayer. Agree with her that, with you and God on her side, everything is going to be all right. After all, that's what friends are for.

Shaped for Service

In the year that King Uzziah died, I saw the Lord sitting on a throne, high and lofty; and the hem of his robe filled the temple. Seraphs were in attendance above him; each had six wings: with two they covered their faces, and with two they covered their feet, and with two they flew. And one called to another and said: "Holy, holy, holy is the Lord of hosts; the whole earth is full of his glory." The pivots on the thresholds shook at the voices of those who called, and the house filled with smoke.

And I said: "Woe is me! I am lost, for I am a man of unclean lips, and I live among a people of unclean lips; yet my eyes have seen the King, the LORD of hosts!" Then one of the seraphs flew to me, holding a live coal that had been taken from the altar with a pair of tongs. The seraph touched my mouth with it and said: "Now that this has touched your lips, your guilt has departed and your sin is blotted out." Then I heard the voice of the Lord saying, "Whom shall I send, and who will go for us?" And I said, "Here am I; send me!" (Isaiah 6:1-8)

You Have an Assignment

Jeremiah 1:1-4

I remember vividly a conversation I had with God about my destination in life. I was a junior in college, without a clue about what God had planned for me. I had no idea what on earth I had been born to be or do.

During that encounter, God made it clear that I was to be a preacher. "A preacher," I thought. "I can't be a preacher. I'm a woman!" At the time, I didn't know and hadn't even heard or seen any female preachers. As far as I was concerned, there was no such thing as a female preacher. Indeed, most of the world, including me, believed that women shouldn't be preachers.

I am sure that it is fairly evident to God that I am a woman! Anyone who sees me can tell I'm a woman. Yet, based on my experience, I believed at the time that my being a woman was a reasonable excuse for me not to heed God's call to preach. In fact, in my mind, my excuse seemed more reasonable than most.

Accept No Excuses

Surely, I am not the only person who has ever used excuses not to answer when God calls. Lots of us use flimsy excuses for not wanting to fulfill our destinies, for not becoming all God has made us to be or called us to do. Indeed, the Bible is full of accounts of persons who had an excuse for why they couldn't do what God wanted them to do. Take Jeremiah, for example. Although he became the greatest prophet in Israelite history, Jeremiah was not above making an excuse when God called him.

You see, when God called him, Jeremiah was preparing to be a priest like his father, Hilkiah. The life of a priest was fairly routine and predictable, especially since the duties were all outlined in the Law. Besides, as the son and grandson of priests, Jeremiah knew what priests did. He had anticipated being a priest all his life and had been groomed for the task.

Jeremiah had not anticipated God calling him to be a prophet. Therefore, when God called him, Jeremiah was caught off guard. His life's plans were interrupted. He was taken outside his comfort zone. That's how God operates when God calls a person into a life of service for him.

I know that some of you think that a call is limited to preachers. But, be clear that every one of God's daughters has a call on her life. If you are saved, you have a call. Paul tells us:

> We know that all things work together for good for those who love God, who are called according to his purpose. For those whom he foreknew he also predestined to be conformed to the image of this Son, in order that [she] might be the firstborn within a large family. And those whom he predestined he also called; and those whom he called he also justified; and those whom he justified he also glorified. (Romans 8:28-30)

Ask for Your Assignment

God saved us so that we can each fulfill the purpose for which God created us. We are not here by accident. God has a plan, purpose, and assignment with your name on it that nobody but you can complete.

Some of you have been struggling to determine why you were even born. You may be pondering the significance of your life. You may want to know why God is keeping you here when circumstances and situations could have taken you out a long time ago. You may wonder why God is so patient with you, even when you mess up over and over again. You may want to know why God provides for your every need, even though you don't deserve it. What is so special about you that God moves heaven and earth to see about you? Why does the Spirit work so hard to get and keep your attention focused on God? It's because God loves you and has great things in store for you. It is because God has great plans for you. Already the Lord has a vested interest in you. God is not playing with you. You can't keep dodging the Holy Spirit, pretending not to hear or understand what God wants with you. You have an assignment!

From the moment God saved you, God interrupted your life's journey and put you on a new path. From that very moment, you were placed on a road that would lead you to discover and fulfill your destiny. Now that you are on the road to fulfilling your divine purpose, you must stay in God's face and on your face in prayer. Through prayer, the Spirit reveals God's purpose and direction for your life. Through constant communication with God, we become clear about what God wants us to do.

Cooperate with the Call

What are you supposed to do after you discover God's purpose for your life? That's simple: cooperate. Opportunity requires obedience. Life would be so much simpler if God's daughters would just do what God asks instead of hemming and hawing, messing around, playing games, wasting time, asking questions, and making excuses.

We are some excuse-making people. But don't worry; we're in good company. Jeremiah was an excuse maker, too. You see, when God called Jeremiah, the first thing out of Jeremiah's mouth was an excuse: "Ah, Lord God, Truly I do not know how to speak, for I am only a boy" (Jeremiah 1:6). In case any of you thinks being a child is a good excuse, you need to know that the word for *boy* or *child* used in the original Hebrew text refers to an age range from childhood to young adulthood. Bible scholars estimate that Jeremiah was probably about twenty years old when God called him. Jeremiah's excuse was that he was too young, too inexperienced, and too ill prepared to be a prophet.

When Jeremiah thought about what God was calling him to do, he was undoubtedly afraid. After all, this was no easy assignment. God was calling Jeremiah to speak on the Lord's behalf, not just to Judah, but to the whole world, to be a prophet to the nations.

Whatever God calls you to do is a bigger task than you ever imagined. It's much bigger than anything you can handle on your own. God does not give us assignments that we can accomplish in our own strength. If we could do it all by ourselves, then we wouldn't need God. Remember, we are called to fulfill God's purpose, not ours. God's assignments always require God's participation.

No matter how big or small the task, God doesn't call us to insignificant assignments. Your calling may not seem like a big thing to you, but in God's economy, every assignment is major. God's call has far-reaching implications. We may be called to serve specific people in a specific place and time, but the impact of our ministries should not be underestimated. We can never know the far-reaching impact of teaching or mentoring one child. The child that you are having the most trouble with today may be a preacher, a teacher, the governor of the state, or the president of the United States tomorrow.

You don't know what an impact fulfilling your destiny will have on the world. We never know how many lives will be saved through helping one sister understand her dignity and worth, and through helping her find employment and a place to live. No one can see how far you will go in the business that God is prompting you to start, the ministry God is birthing in your spirit, the work God has placed in your hand. Who knows how many families will reconcile through your counseling, intervention, and prayers. I never envisioned that the call to preach that God placed on my life some thirty-five years ago would have landed me where God has me today.

What's Stopping You?

For me, the call of God was so awesome that I felt overwhelmed. I was afraid, and I felt inadequate. Excuses often mask our feelings and fear of inadequacy. Yet we must never underestimate what God wants to do. After all, the God who calls us is the sovereign God of the world. We may not feel up to the task, but the God who calls us is.

So, what's your excuse? Is it your lack of education? Perhaps you dropped out or got kicked out and never went back. Is it that you feel you haven't achieved much with your life and think your life has no value, meaning, or worth when compared with others? From your perspective, perhaps your life doesn't count. But God says, "For surely I know the plans I have for you, says the LORD, plans for your welfare and not for harm, to give you a future with hope" (Jeremiah 29:11). What's stopping you from going back to school to get the degree or training you need to fulfill your destiny? You may doubt your ability to make it in school. Know that with God, all things are possible. As Philippians 4:13 reminds us, you can do all things and anything through Christ who gives you strength.

Perhaps you are not as young as you once were, not as agile or vital as you used to be. You may believe that your time is past and that you have missed your opportunity. Perhaps you failed to discover your purpose when you were younger, or perhaps you knew but were afraid to try, and now you think it's too late. Know that it's never too late. Age is nothing but a number. Don't let your age, no matter how old or how young, stop you from whatever God wants for you.

What is time to God? God is the Ancient of Days, the Alpha and the Omega. When you are in Christ, your life is measured by eternity. When Sarah gave birth to Isaac after decades of infertility, she was way past the childbearing age. God's wonders know no time.

What's your excuse? You may already have a degree and a high-powered job and are living quite comfortably, so it seems. Your job may be just a job to you. Perhaps, it is something you chose but not what God has chosen for you! God keeps trying to move you out of your comfort zone and into your assignment, but maybe you aren't ready to move because you are afraid. Many of us are quick to doubt ourselves and to question our ability to handle certain responsibilities, even when we are already in positions of authority. We can be running the show but still feel inadequate. We allow others' opinions, our past failures, and underestimating our abilities and resources to cause us to fear even trying to fulfill God's call upon our lives. Some of us are afraid to discover our purpose, because we are already convinced that we can't possibly fulfill it.

Some of us are allowing our pasts to keep us from moving into our futures. You may be allowing the enemy to convince you that you can never overcome your past and never measure up and become adequate in God's sight. Satan is a liar. Indeed, as John 8:44 warns us, Satan is the father of lies. If you are saved, you have already overcome your past in and through Christ Jesus. In Christ, your past is forgiven and forgotten, and your future possibilities and opportunities are assured and secured.

God Knows It All

Your excuses will not work in God's realm. They never will and never have. God countered all of Jeremiah's and our excuses with a wonderful assurance: *I know you*. And God didn't get to know Jeremiah at the moment he called him. Jeremiah 1:5 states, "Before I formed you in the womb I knew you, and before you were born I consecrated you; I appointed you a prophet to the nations."

God knows who you are and what you are. God knows everything about you. The Hebrew word for "know" is *yada*, meaning "to have intimate knowledge of another." God knows us intimately. God knows everything there is to know about us: the good, the bad, and the ugly. God knows the things we keep hoping no one will find out, the things we wish we could forget but can't seem to, God knows. God knows our abilities and capabilities and our strengths and weaknesses. God knows our successes and failures. God knows all about our insecurities and our feelings of inadequacy.

When God calls you, God isn't surprised when you show up with all your baggage in tow. God chose you before the foundation of the world, before you were even thought about, long before you made your first mistake. God knew you wouldn't be perfect. When God chose you, despite your imperfections, God made that choice in full knowledge of who you are and what you have done.

Like Jeremiah, before you were even conceived, God had a plan for your life. God already knew the purpose for which you would be born. God didn't have to wait until you were born to see what talents and abilities you would have to lend to our assignment.

God knew exactly what you would need to be the person to fulfill the purpose for which you were created. In effect God says, "I have created you to carry out the work I myself am placing in your hands to do. You lack nothing that you need to achieve my divine purpose for your life."

Be clear that the gifts and abilities you have been given are not for yourself. Like Jeremiah, before you were born, God knew you, but God also set you apart. You cannot be whatever you want to be. Our human tendency is to control our lives however we want. You see, before we were born, we were shaped and formed in the womb by God for God's own purpose and for God's own glory.

Perhaps you are wondering why you are not fully satisfied with the life you are choosing to live. It's because you have been set apart! You want to know why the people, places, and things you think you needed to be happy aren't living up to your expectations. You are wondering why the job you thought you would die if you didn't get is now killing you. It's because you are holy, sanctified, and set apart. You can't be anything you want to be. You can't do anything you want to do. You can't live any way you want to live, because you are not your own. You are set apart, and you have an assignment!

With that knowledge, there is only one thing left for you. Do what God tells you to do. God has provided you with everything you need to complete the assignment. And what you don't have, God will provide that, too! Tell God, "OK. Have your own way in my life."

You have an assignment! What are you waiting for? Step to it! Enter into your destiny!

A Woman of Influence

Judges 4:1-10

Do you know how powerful and influential you are? Most women don't. When we think about powerful women, we tend to think of elected officials, well-positioned sisters in corporate America, or those with degrees from the finest schools in the country. We tend to think of powerful women as those who have corner offices and six-figure incomes or those who have extensive influence through celebrity status as politicians, entertainers, talk show hosts, or best-selling authors.

But when I speak of powerful women, I mean something quite different. The type of powerful woman of whom I speak may be well-off or just coming off welfare. She may be well connected or just barely getting herself together. She may hold multiple degrees or have on-the-job experience. She may be married or single, young or old. Everyone may know her name, or she may be known only by a precious few.

For, you see, all women are powerful. All women have influence. It's in our nature. God wired us that way. We've just got it like that! Don't believe me? Consider these biblical women and the influence they had on their world—and ours!

- Ask Eve, who offered her husband forbidden fruit, and he ate it.
- Ask Rahab, who saved herself and her family from destruction when the walls of Jericho fell.
- Ask Ruth, a Moabite, who married Boaz, a Jew, and became a part of Jesus' bloodline.

- Ask Esther, a peasant girl who became a Persian queen and had the king veto his own law to save her people.
- Ask Mary, whose son Jesus turned water into wine at a wedding, against his wishes and at her request.
- Ask the Syro-Phoenician woman whose daughter Jesus healed upon her insistence.
- Ask Lois, whose son Timothy became a faithful disciple of Christ and Paul as well as a minister of the gospel, even though his father was a heathen.

The Power of Relationship

These were all power-packing women, for sure, and so are you. But what is the source of our power as women? It is the influence that we carry in relationships. God designed us to value and nurture relationships. Therefore, it is through relationships that we carve out our spheres of influence. Every person with whom we come into contact is influenced by us in one way or another.

One of our most important spheres of influence is created through relationships with our children. Many years ago, the poet William Ross Wallace wrote a poem entitled "The Hand That Rocks the Cradle Is the Hand That Rules the World." That is so true. Although a lot of fathers are involved in raising their children, in most instances, mothers have a more intimate and impressible relationship with their children.

Women are the makers of kings and queens, presidents and governors, senators and congresspersons, persons who sit in the highest seats of power across this nation and world. The boy-child you are raising could be governor one day. The little girl you are mentoring may be destined to become a member of Congress, the Senate, or even president of the United States. The child who is giving you a fit in the classroom could be the greatest author, athlete, preacher, or teacher who ever lived, all because of your influence!

So what is influence? According to Merriam-Webster's Collegiate Dictionary, it is "the power or capacity of causing an effect in indirect or intangible ways." Because influence has the quality of being indirect or unapparent, it is possible that we influence the attitudes and actions of persons without even realizing it.

Consider again your influence on children. They may say things or display attitudes at a very young age that leave you wondering where they learned to say or do that. I can't tell you exactly where they learned it, but I know who taught them: you did. In many ways, children become mirror images of their mothers and fathers, often unbeknown to the parents. It's all about influence!

No matter our station in life, each one of us has a sphere of influence. God has designed us to have unparalleled influence and power in people's lives, especially after we have become God's daughters! We are called to make a difference in whatever sphere of influence we have been afforded: in our homes, on our jobs, at church, in the community, at our children's schools, among our friends and associates, sometimes among people we don't even know.

The Significance of Shortcomings

You may never have seen yourself as a powerful woman, much less an influential one. You may not feel worthy of this high calling. You may not yet fully understand who you are, your dignity and worth, the fact that you are invaluable to God and to the world, even before considering the power and influence you hold.

As women we often struggle to see anything special or significant about ourselves. In our minds, we are just ordinary. If we were not born rich and famous, have not made newsworthy contributions to society, or have not received any honors that would distinguish us, we wonder why in the world God would want to use us.

You may be thinking: I have not lived a life that would impress God or anyone else. I came from the 'hood! I still live in the 'hood. My past is shameful at best. If people knew who I really am after I take off my makeup, if they only knew the things I have done and where I came from, they wouldn't like me, much less listen to me. Me? Influential? Please!

Don't you know who you are? Well, let me remind you that you are no longer who or what you used to be. Now that you know Christ, a wonderful change has taken place in your life. Your many sins have all been washed away. Therefore, you don't need to run and hide from your past. The apostle Paul says:

Consider your own call, . . . sisters: not many of you were wise by human standards, not many were powerful, not many were of noble birth. But God chose what is foolish in the world to shame the wise; God chose what is weak in the world to shame the strong; God chose what is low and despised in the world, things that are not, to reduce to nothing things that are, so that no one might boast in the presence of God. (1 Corinthians 1:26-29)

What you see as liabilities are the very things that make you appealing to God. Your so-called shortcomings qualify you for God's special attention and promotion. God takes sinners and makes saints. God takes ordinary people and makes us extraordinary. God takes people who are picked over, pushed aside, put down, rejected, and neglected and makes us jewels fit for a crown.

You may see yourself as cut glass, but God sees a diamond in the rough. You may see yourself as an insignificant grain of sand, but God sees a pearl in process. Never underestimate who and what you can become when you yield yourself to God. In Christ, we are made worthy and complete. We lack nothing to answer God's call to influence and to make a difference in the world. As we surrender, God "is able to accomplish abundantly far more than all we can ever ask or imagine" (Ephesians 3:20). God wants to use you to impact and transform this present world into the realm of God, simply by operating in your sphere of influence.

You may not realize it, but you can help save the world by ensuring that your child or any child has a healthy self-perception, is confident and self-assured. You can change the world by encouraging the man in your life to live up to his fullest potential. You can help catapult your sisters into places they never dreamed possible with your affirmation, support, and appreciation of their gifts and abilities. Powerful and influential women working together in partnership with the others can make things happen. We can turn this world right side up and inside out!

A Woman to Be Reckoned With

The Bible is full of stories of powerful and influential women who made things happen. Their stories provide examples to edify and encourage women of today to step out of the shadows and seize the moment and opportunities for which we have been destined. Their stories instruct us how to become women of influence.

One such woman is Deborah. Deborah was truly a force to be reckoned with. The only female judge in Israel (at least as far as we know from Scripture), Deborah ruled during a time when Israel was spiritually bankrupt because they had repeatedly rebelled against and had rejected God. When the Lord got tired of them, God turned them over to Jabin, a Canaanite king, and to the commander of Jabin's army, Sisera, who cruelly oppressed the Israelites for twenty years.

Deborah, whose name means "the bee," had no aristocratic heritage or royal lineage. All the Scriptures say about her personally was that she was the wife of Lappidoth. Though she called herself "a mother in Israel" (Judges 5:7), apparently Deborah didn't have children of her own. From all appearances, she was an ordinary woman. Yet God called her to do extraordinary things.

Deborah had two very special callings. First, she was a prophet—a mouthpiece for God. God used her to speak God's will to the people. Deborah was also a judge. Every day "she used to sit under the palm of Deborah between Ramah and Bethel in the hill country of Ephraim; and the Israelites came up to her for judgment" (Judges 4:5).

Judge and prophet: That is a powerful and influential combination. Not only was Deborah endowed with the ability to discern the mind and will of God and declare it to others, but she was also in the position to use the messages God sent her to advise the people who sought her counsel. You see, prophets had a special relationship with God, an intimate relationship that took precedence over and yet informed all the other relationships. Her special relationship allowed her to give special counsel. Deborah received divine wisdom during her intimate times with God. Because of her intimate relationship, Deborah could give the people wisdom from God, not simply her opinion or what sounded good and right.

The Power of Knowing God

While every powerful and influential woman does not have to be a prophet, she does need to have an intimate relationship with God. She needs to continually seek God's counsel and wisdom. Speaking and listening to God regularly allows God constantly to reveal things. You don't have to wonder about anything. You don't need to be confused or concerned about making the right choices. You don't have to struggle too hard to figure out the major or minor details of your life. God will tell you everything you need to know when you need to know it. God says, "Call to me and I will answer you, and tell you great and hidden things that you have not known" (Jeremiah 33:3).

The Hebrew word *batsar* is translated in the New Revised Standard Version as "hidden". Other English Bibles render it as "unsearchable". The Hebrew means "inaccessible," that which was not previously known and can only be revealed by God. God wants to reveal some things to you that will absolutely blow your mind. People are depending upon you to hear from God so that you can counsel them into reaching their destiny.

A number of people may come to you daily for advice and counsel about what they should do, how to handle certain situations, how they should feel about some injustice or mistreatment. They may ask you what to do about a relationship that is on the rocks, a marriage that has grown cold, a child who is "tripping" and out of control, or a situation on the job or at school. Your sister-girlfriends need to be able to depend on you for solid advice and counsel. Your husband should be able to trust what you say. Although they won't admit it, your children and grandchildren, nieces and nephews already think you know everything and can solve any problem, which is why they keep coming to you for advice. Do you see how much influence you have?

People at your job watch your every move; the people around you hang on your every word. They are checking you out to see how you act and react, what is important to you, how you conduct your business and pleasure. They know who you are. They can see it in your walk, hear it in your talk. They observe the way you carry yourself. They see you as having the answers they have been looking for. They want to glean from your wisdom, follow your direction. They keep coming to you because they have confidence in you.

I am going to say it again: You are a powerful and influential woman. For that reason, when you speak, you need to have the Word of God in your mouth and not just something you read in a magazine or heard from your favorite talk-show personality.

We can give people worldly wisdom, or we can give them the wisdom of God. We need to be strong women who will stand for what is right and consistently live a life of love and godly witness. The world needs women who have a heart for God and the things of God. In times like these, when there are no absolutes and everyone is doing what seems right in their own eyes, people need to hear a word of hope, peace, and direction. They need a word from the Lord!

But in order to stand, we will need to have an intimate relationship with God. God needs time set aside just for the two of you. Whether it is early in the morning, late at night, at noonday, or in the middle of the night, call on God. Whatever time you pick, God is available to you. Allow God to whisper sweet *every*things in your ear. The Spirit will make God's presence known during those intimate times in ways that allow you to prosper and become all that God has destined you to be.

The Power of Being Passionate

In addition to having an intimate relationship with God, a woman of influence must also be impassioned. Passion is a gift from God. Our passion for God and for God's will in our lives grows as we spend intimate times with the Lord! Passion is the pure motivation to respond to the needs of others as you are uniquely gifted to do. God reveals and solidifies our passions through the desires of our hearts, the circumstances of our lives, and God's confirming Word. Have you been divorced, depressed, unemployed, grief-stricken, or abused? Your past struggles are often areas where God will develop a passion within you. God delivers us to deliver others who are bound in the ways we have been bound, whose struggles are similar to ours, whose messes match ours.

You see, the messy places—those places that have bound you—are often the areas where you can learn to minister most effectively and most passionately. Your place of passion is where you will have the greatest influence and impact in the world. When we women are passionate about something, it won't let us go and we won't let it go. We cannot put it down when we want, leave it alone until a more convenient time, or shake it off because it is uncomfortable.

Some of us hesitate to become passionate about the things God has called us to do. We may be afraid that we will become too consumed by the passion, overwhelmed by the burden or the challenge of the call. Certainly there is that risk, but God doesn't call influential women to minor, insignificant assignments that require no personal sacrifice or involvement. It is, therefore, appropriate for us to get caught up in our passions.

Another reason some of us hesitate to embrace God's calling is that we feel inadequate for the task. But we must remember, God equips whomever God calls. In fact, we were equipped the moment we were created. God is simply waiting for us to tap into the passion already placed in us.

Deborah was passionate about the deliverance of Israel. Her passion led her to be compassionate about the struggles and oppression of her people. It was her passion to save her people that caused her to leave the comfort of being a homemaker and allowed God to promote her to a judge and ruler of Israel. God used Deborah's passion and influence to deliver the people of Israel. As the Lord did with Deborah, God will use our passion in accomplishing the deliverance of others.

The Power of Working Together

Finally, a woman of influence has to be interdependent. We have to be able to work with people. We cannot fly solo. We are to operate in our giftedness with humility while also valuing the gifts of others. Interdependence allows us to stand in the gap for others and for others to stand in the gap for us when we have given up. Consider again Deborah's story. God told Deborah to tell the man Barak to take ten thousand men of Naphtali and Zebulun and lead the way to Mount Tabor. There God would deliver Sisera, the enemy commander, into Barak's hands. That may not seem like a difficult task, unless you consider that Sisera had one hundred thousand men and nine hundred chariots.

When Deborah told Barak what the Lord had instructed, Barak was afraid. He did not want to go to Mount Tabor to take on Sisera and his army—not unless Deborah went with him. We have all been in situations when those around us could not see what God has made clear to us. They have struggled to believe, trust, and obey God, especially under seemingly impossible circumstances. Despite the fact that God promised to deliver Sisera into Barak's hands, Barak refused to go it alone. He trusted that God's hand was on Deborah and believed that he needed to lean on her to see himself through.

Like Deborah, at times, we have to be willing to go with people to places where they are not willing to go alone and to have faith when they have none. Women, especially mothers, have always done this! Mothers believe in us when we do not believe in ourselves. They believe God for us when we struggle to believe. A mother's faith has saved many of us delivered us from addictions, healed us from broken marriages and unhealthy relationships, seen us graduate from institutions we didn't even think we could get into, and watched us work in positions for which people said we were not qualified.

Like Deborah, we must also accept people unconditionally for who they are and where they are in life, and we must be patient with them. This requires that we let go of unrealistic expectations of others and let them mature at their own pace, not the pace we believe they should take. Deborah didn't judge Barak's fear or his lack of faith. Rather she understood where he was and supported him.

At times, we must tolerate much more than we bargained for in our relationships with others. Our expectations of people often do not match our experiences with them. This can be disappointing and frustrating to say the least. But you ought to know by now that you cannot make someone be who and what he or she is not. You must recognize who and where that person is.

Someone you love may seem obstinate to the faith or slow to do what he or she needs to do. Love that person; don't nag. Pray for that person; don't plague him or her. If faith and confidence in God are evident in your life, sooner or later that fact will influence them. Your friends may be losing their minds, but when they see how you handle the storms of life in quietness and confidence, you will influence them to want what you have.

There are people all around you who long to be delivered from the demons that oppress them day and night; they long to know the joy that you know. They may not discover their purposes or pursue their destinies unless you go with them to show the way.

Here's how Deborah's story ends: Armed with confidence in God, Deborah went with Barak to fight against Sisera. Deborah used her influence to help Barak gather the men he needed. When he advanced, the Lord routed Sisera and his whole army, and the army was defeated. The troops of Sisera fell by the swords of men, but a woman drove a stake through Sisera's own head and killed him (Judges 4:21). On that day, God subdued the Canaanite king before the Israelites. And the hand of the Israelites grew stronger and stronger until they destroyed their enemy. "And the land had rest forty years" (Judges 5:31).

God is calling each one of us to be a woman of influence, just as God called Deborah. As we spend intimate time with God, embracing our God-given passions and recognizing that others depend upon us and we on others, God will use our influence to deliver others from their oppression into a life of victory and peace. Don't you know who you are? Woman of power, exert your God-given influence!

A Woman of Excellence

Acts 16:13-15

In Acts, chapter 16, we find the apostle Paul and his companions in the middle of their second missionary journey, taking the good news of Jesus Christ all over the known world, establishing churches wherever they go in Jesus' name. Having already visited the churches founded during his first journey with Barnabas, Paul desires to proceed to Asia, but the Holy Spirit will not let him leave the area.

So Paul and his crew travel down to Troas and wait for direction on how to proceed. While there, Paul has a vision of a man begging him to "come over to Macedonia and help us" (Acts 16:9). Concluding that the Lord has directed them to preach the gospel in Macedonia, Paul and his companions leave immediately. From Troas they sail to Samothrace, then to Neapolis, and finally they arrive at their destination, Philippi.

Philippi was a Roman colony, a prosperous trade center, and the leading city of that district in Macedonia. Although Paul's stay in Philippi is relatively brief compared to the other places he visits, Paul's letter to the church there seems to indicate that it was one of the most memorable places he visited. While there, Paul not only establishes a dynamic church, but also meets some women of excellence, one of whom is Lydia.

On the Sabbath, Paul and his companions go outside the city gate looking for a place of prayer. A place of prayer was the alternative for worship in a city that did not have enough men to establish a Jewish congregation. According to Jewish law, ten male heads of household in regular attendance were necessary to establish a congregation. If a congregation could not be established, a place of prayer outdoors, often near a river or another body of water, was to be arranged.

At one of these places of prayer, Paul finds a group of women gathered. Apparently no men were there that day; the text doesn't comment on their absence. But the women were there, worshiping and adoring God, undoubtedly praying and exhorting one another with the words of the *Shema*, the Jewish affirmation of faith, which declares:

> Hear, O Israel! The LORD is our God, the LORD alone.
> You shall love the LORD your God with all your heart
> and with all your soul and with all your might. (Deuteronomy 6:4-5, Tanakh)

The women were seeking God's heart, encouraging one another to wholehearted devotion to him, reading from the Law and the Prophets, and expecting a blessing. And, because I know what can happen when women of God get together to worship, I know that the place where Paul found Lydia and the other women was a powerful place.

I don't know what it is about women getting together to worship. Jesus promised that when two or three gather in his name, he will be in their midst. He didn't specify whether those two or three had to be men or women. But I declare that more than you could ever hope for or imagine happens when women of faith assemble in one place, lifting up holy hands and hearts, seeking God!

When we worship, we acknowledge the perfection, majesty, and divine sovereignty of God, giving glory to the Lord who alone is worthy. We stand before God in adoration with a sense of awe and wonder, being consumed by God's presence. We take our eyes off ourselves and our problems to concentrate on God. When women worship God, the atmosphere is changed and charged, our prayers and praise rise as a fragrant offering, a sweet-smelling savor before the very throne of God. The Lord inhabits our praises. God becomes up-close and personal. The stage is set for God to move in unprecedented ways in our midst. Yes, when we women worship, there is something special in the air.

Lydia, a successful businesswoman, was a woman whose home became a meeting place for early Christians. Paul and his companions were guests in that home. I would suggest that those times of gathering provided her with the fuel she needed to become a woman of excellence. Therefore, we sisters can take a page from Lydia's book on how to become women of excellence.

Woman of Prayer

First of all, Lydia was a woman of excellence because she was a woman of prayer. She was a woman of faith even before she heard the gospel of Jesus from Paul. Her life was so immersed in worship that not only did she respond immediately to Paul's preaching, but her entire household responded in faith and joined her in baptism. Lydia undoubtedly knew the power and effect of worship because she made a daily commitment to be in that place of prayer to offer her worship to God. If we are to become women of excellence, then, like Lydia, we too must be faithful in prayer.

In this crazy, mixed-up, and unsettled world, we need to understand the value of prayer as never before. Too often we sing and shout but then go out and try to handle things on our own. We forget or underestimate the power of prayer in our worship and in our workaday lives. We spend too much time being frustrated about situations that are beyond our control. As women, we sometimes feel powerless and think that our only recourse is to fuss, cuss, nag, get all bent out of shape, or "show out" with folks to get them to see our point of view or do what we want them to do. We must remember that we are in the world but not of it. We need to spend less time talking to others and more time talking with God.

When women of faith stop talking to one another and start praying to God, something extraordinary, absolutely incredible, and mind-blowing happens. When women pray, lives are changed and rearranged. When women pray, broken hearts and homes are put back together again. When women pray, people are set free, saved, healed, and delivered. When we pray, God assigns angels to our case. As we pray, heaven intersects with earth, releasing power and possibility that allow us to handle situations and demolish strongholds.

When we pray, we take hold of the authority Jesus granted to us: "I will give you the keys of the kingdom of heaven, and whatever you bind on earth will be bound in heaven, and whatever you loose on earth will be loosed in heaven" (Matthew 16:19). When we pray, God is able to do immeasurably more than we can ask for or imagine, according to God's power that is at work within us (Ephesians 3:20).

Women of excellence are women who have learned the power of prayer. They have learned, as their grandmothers probably knew, that having a little talk with Jesus can make it right. They have learned that without prayer, we forfeit peace and bear pains needlessly, to paraphrase the hymnwriter Joseph Scriven. There is, indeed, power in our prayers. If we are to be women of excellence, we must pray diligently.

Woman in Partnership

Lydia's life also shows us that women of excellence are women who partner with other women. She wasn't praying and worshiping at that river alone. She was there in the company of other women, women of her household and probably other women of the city. They would have known her, Lydia, the dealer in fine purple cloth, a prosperous entrepreneur who had status and respect in the community. Lydia evidently valued the company of other women.

Some things happen in our lives that only another woman can understand. No one but a sister can understand our various moods. Only another woman, particularly one who loves us and is a committed friend, wants to hear all the drama that is happening in our lives. When we are going through a crisis, are hurting, or have been wounded or disappointed, we need someone who will tarry with us, listen to us for hours, even days, as we go over every detail of our problem or pain. No one can feel our pain like a sister. No one else can tell us when we are wrong and when we have cried long enough and when it's time to move on. When you are friends with a woman of excellence, you don't have to play games. In fact, you can't play games. Try to impress her. Don't act as if you have it all together when you really don't. She knows the real deal. You can let your guard down and just be yourself.

Friendships and fellowship with other women are essential to our lives. Sisterhood is a powerful force and resource. So, let us stop the petty competition, backbiting, hating, and hurting one another. Instead, let us begin to cooperate with, affirm, and support one another. If you want to be a woman of excellence, you need to find time to connect with other women who are on their way to being a women of excellence like you.

Lydia and the other women partnered in praise and worship at a time when it was not in vogue to be worshipers of God. Becoming a Christian was more dangerous yet because the new believers didn't enjoy even the limited protection that Jews did under the Roman Empire. These women partnered at a time when women were considered particularly helpless and vulnerable. They must have known that having God and each other to lean on would make everything all right. As we work together with our sisters in Jesus' name, God will make it all right with us, too.

Woman of Purpose

Lydia was also a woman of purpose who knew how to take care of business. The text states she was a dealer in purple cloth from the city of Thyatira, which was known for its purple dyes and fabric. Lydia may have been either a representative of one of the sellers that marketed the purple dyes and fabric, or perhaps she had moved to Philippi to promote her own business. Whatever the case, she was a successful businesswoman. Otherwise, she would not have been able to go to the leading city in Macedonia. You had to have it going on to be able to trade in Philippi. Lydia must have exhibited ability, enthusiasm, singleness of purpose, and mental acumen, because she prospered greatly in her profession.

Like Lydia, a woman of excellence operates with high standards, whether she owns her own business or works for someone else. Whether she is a corporate executive, a lawyer, an administrator, a teacher, a homemaker, a cook, a secretary, a hairdresser, or a student still preparing for a profession, a woman of excellence does not play. She knows what she is doing and can handle herself and her responsibilities. A woman of excellence manages her affairs and the affairs of others well. She is indispensable; her work is impeccable, her ability phenomenal. She gets up early to pray and prepare for the challenges of the day. She arrives at work early and leaves late. She attends class every day and masters skills necessary to effectively do her job. Her reports are well written; her presentations are "tight."

At the same time, women do have a tendency to overcommit ourselves. We allow others' expectations to overwhelm us. We become like Martha, the sister of Mary and Lazarus, to whom Jesus said, "You are worried and distracted by many things" (Luke 10:41). Martha was *distracted*, which in Greek means "pulled apart in many directions." This is the opposite of being *focused*, which is "to center one's attention, one's activities on one thing."

Even those of us who are skilled in multitasking can focus on only two or three things at a time and be truly effective. When we are pulled in many directions at once, we frequently make too many commitments, often because we don't know how to say no and mean it. With all the demands of daily living, we must learn to focus on what is most important. Yet many of us let others set our priorities—our parents, children, employers, friends, spouses or boyfriends, even our church families.

We must learn to set our own priorities and focus on the most important things first. A woman of excellence has learned how to have balance in her life. She has learned to focus on what is primary and leave or delegate the rest to someone else. A woman of excellence focuses on her priorities and lives her life according to her God-given purpose.

Woman Who Prospers

Like Lydia, a woman of excellence is also prosperous. Lydia understood that God had given her skills and abilities to produce wealth, and she was maximizing her potential. You see, the purple dye and fabric she sold were quite expensive. Lydia's clients had to be well-off to purchase her goods. No doubt, Lydia was paid a royal fee for her royal purple.

Sisters, we too must be paid what we are worth. Unless God has led you into missions, a street ministry, or some other vocation that doesn't pay well, you need to choose a profession that will allow you to build wealth. We can no longer afford to work jobs from sunup to sundown, doing the same work as everyone else and getting paid less. God wants to use you to finance the work of God's earthly realm, but you can't do it if you are broke.

Some of you know that you are being paid less than what you are worth. If you need to go back to school or update your résumé and find a better-paying job, do it. If you are qualified and doing the work but not getting paid, make an appointment with your supervisor to help him or her understand how much you are worth.

If we want to be prosperous, we need to make sure we get paid what we're worth, and we don't need to spend every dime we make. For many of us, money burns a hole in our pockets, so instead of saving some, we spend it all. When we don't have cash on hand, we often buy on credit, and before we know it, we owe more than we can afford to pay back in a lifetime.

Truth be told, we have nothing of any real value to show for our indebtedness. We charge items like perfume, body creams, and stockings. Sister, you cannot build wealth paying exorbitant interest on credit cards, making minimum payments of twenty dollars on a three-thousand-dollar bill. You can't build wealth when you owe all you make to Macy's, T.J. Maxx, or Target.

A woman of excellence has learned the importance of working for what she is worth. She gives to her church in tithes and offerings. She buys with cash, and she also saves, invests, and builds wealth through amassing appreciating assets, such as houses and land. Are you gainfully employed and reasonably settled in your current city but still paying rent on an apartment? Buy a house! Stop irresponsible spending and living!

Develop a plan for debt-free living, and work your plan. Keep only one credit card for convenience, and cut up the rest. We don't know whether Lydia was married at this point in her life, but we do know that she had a house big enough to accommodate Paul and all his companions. Lydia was prosperous not only because her profession allowed her to create wealth, but because she seemed to have known how to manage the money she had. Like Lydia, if we are to prosper as women of excellence, we must learn to be good managers of the resources that God provides.

Woman in Pursuit

Finally, Lydia was a woman of excellence because she was in hot pursuit of God. When we meet her in Acts 16, she is in worship. Even though Lydia was a successful businesswoman, she still realized she needed something money can't buy. She knew she needed someone who could add real meaning to her life. Lydia's faithful and passionate pursuit of God was apparently so evident that Paul and his male companions were willing to risk social censure by becoming guests in her home.

Like the Samaritan woman whom Jesus met at the well, Lydia had an insatiable desire that could only be filled with the Living Water. She pursued the one who satisfies an unquenchable thirst down on the inside. There is an empty place inside each of us that hangs on like gnawing grief. It may be brought on by unhealthy choices, by the absence of a satisfying relationship, or by life's challenges in general. Only God can fill this empty place inside of us.

Knowing this, Lydia ran after the one who would keep her focused amid conflicting priorities, grant her wisdom in the decisions of household and business, and sustain her when the demands of life wore her down. Like Lydia, if you run to God for whatever you need. God will give another chance when you have messed up and lost your way. When you are frustrated and wondering if life is worth living, God will reach out to you and hold you close. When you feel empty and alone, God will pour into you the Holy Spirit and satisfy your longings as no one else can. God is a Master at filling empty space.

You may have already accepted Christ as your Savior, but perhaps you still don't feel whole, complete, or satisfied. You may still be living a restless and reckless life, looking for love in all the wrong places, searching for meaning in meaningless ways. You may feel as if something is missing. You may wonder if there is something more to life or if this is as good as it gets. Remember this: Jesus came that you might have life and that more abundantly (John 10:10)! God wants you to live a full life with purpose and meaning. God wants you to live the extraordinary life that Jesus promised when you accepted him into your heart.

Some of your life's plans may not have been fulfilled. Some things in your life may not have come together as you thought they would. Perhaps you thought you'd be married by now, that you'd have children or a degree or that promotion you have been working for. You just figured you would be further along in your life. Your reality is falling short of your expectations. But don't give up. Remember, God has plans for you, good plans, plans to prosper you and not harm you, plans to give you hope and a future of excellence (Jeremiah 29:11).

God has promised, "When you call upon me and come and pray to me, I will hear you. When you search for me, you will find me; if you seek me with all your heart" (Jeremiah 29:12-13). Most of us know how to go after what we want, even those of us who are otherwise quiet and unassuming. If we see something we want, we will move everything in our way to get to it. God wants to be your first love forever! God wants to be your everything. Nobody can love you or take care of you like God can. No one can satisfy you like God can.

If we truly want to be fulfilled, we have to go after God and the things of God with reckless abandon through worship, study of the Word, prayer, and praise. We have to run after God with a passion that is not easily squelched. We have to be as available to

God as we are to everyone else. A woman of excellence will stop at nothing to pursue God.

When Lydia sought God at that prayer meeting, she received a deeper revelation of God through Jesus Christ. God opened her heart and poured in the very Spirit of God. When you get just as serious about seeking God with all your heart as Lydia was, you, too, will find God. The Lord will give you everything you have been searching for. You will find purpose and prosperity. God will make your life brand-new and will fill you with greater joy than you have ever known. And you will become God's woman of excellence.

It's Time

Esther 4:12-17

Biblical stories of women whom God called out of obscurity to do mighty exploits on God's behalf are few and far between. Nevertheless, they are there!

- Sarah gave birth to a nation;
- Deborah became Israel's only female judge;
- Esther saved her people from extinction during the Persian exile;
- Mary bore in her womb the Savior of the world; and
- Lydia, a savvy businesswoman, became the first European convert to Christ and then lead many to him.

These women never intended to be or do anything great. They were ordinary women, just like you and me, trying to make a living and a life, until God called them out of the shadows and positioned them to effect change in the world and in the lives of people. All of these women were simply minding their own business, when suddenly they found themselves in the spotlight changing the very course of history. Let me show you what I mean.

Sarah was a barren woman who wanted a child to legitimate her womanhood. She believed the promise of God that her nonagenarian husband, Abraham, would have a son. She laughed aloud when God allowed her to become mother of that child. Little did she realize that Isaac would be the link to a nation from which the Savior of the world would come.

Deborah was the wife of Lappidoth. That is the only fact that Scripture reveals about Deborah—except the exhilarating story about how she served God as a judge and prophet and led Israel in war during a tumultuous time in its history.

Mary was a poor, teenaged virgin hanging out in Nazareth when the angel of the Lord told her she was highly favored and would give birth to God's Son. She became mother of the promised Messiah and one of Jesus' most faithful disciples.

Lydia was an ambitious and enterprising businesswoman whose faithfulness impressed even the apostle Paul. She was the first European to embrace the Good News of Jesus, and God used her to spread the gospel and grow the church.

And as we will see, Esther was an orphan girl who was recruited to enter a beauty contest to become a Persian queen, and who eventually saved her people from genocide.

Yes, God can use anyone at any time, even you as you contemplate the meaning of this existence, wondering if your life matters given some of the messes you have made. Yes, while you think about the time you have wasted in unproductive activity, trying to figure out who you are and if you have what it takes to be someone great, God is working in your heart as well as behind the scenes to position you to fulfill the purpose for which you were created. God knows how to redeem wasted time and can make something good out of even the most messed-up situations.

You may be one of those people whose life is on track. Everything is going according your plan. In that case, you need to know that you are a prime candidate for God to interrupt your flow and turn your life in another direction. Out of nowhere, an opportunity may arise that you just cannot ignore. When it's your time, you should not dare to let the opportunity pass, because it may never come again. You must seize the moments when God wants to use you for a divine purpose—to bring glory to God and to be a blessing to God's people. The Lord's plan may not be what you have in mind, but you have been on God's mind before you were formed you in the womb (Jeremiah 1:5).

Like Sarah, Deborah, Mary, Lydia, and Esther, you were placed on this earth to fulfill a specific call at a specified time. Some of you already know this, but you just don't want to believe it. God has told you by waking you up early in the morning or by whispering to you in the middle of sermons and Bible study. You may want to keep on dodging the call, but you can only evade God for so long. One day, God will place you between a rock and a hard place, where you will be forced to decide to heed God's call at God's time.

That is the exactly what happened to Esther, a Jewish girl whose real name was Hadassah. Hadassah was a Jewish exile living in the Persian Empire during the reign of Artaxerxes. She was an orphan who had been adopted and raised by her cousin, Mordecai, son of Jair of the house of Benjamin.

At the beginning of his reign, Artaxerxes threw a seven-day party during which he commanded his wife, Queen Vashti, to come out so that he could display her beauty. When Vashti refused, the king essentially divorced her and exiled her from the kingdom. Artaxerxes' personal attendants proposed that they make a careful search of all the beautiful young virgins to find him a new queen. A call went throughout the land, and beautiful young girls were brought into the harem of the king, placed under the care of Hegai, the king's eunuch. One of those young women brought to the king's palace was Hadassah, Mordecai's cousin. Mordecai had forbidden Hadassah to reveal her Jewish nationality, so she was given the Persian name Esther, which means, "star."

And what a star she was. When it was Esther's turn to go to the king, she had already won the favor of the caretaker, Hegai, and everyone else who saw her. She was beautiful physically and had a lovely personality. Before Esther was even presented to the king, God's hand was already at work.

Although God's name is never mentioned in the biblical book that tells Esther's story, God's providence is evident on every page. Why would a Jewish cousin want his young charge to marry a heathen king? Providence. How is it that when she was placed in Hegai's care, out of four hundred others, Esther pleased him and won his favor? Providence.

The providence of God. It was God who orchestrated the details of Esther's life. On the surface, Esther's story may appear to be about a beauty contest, but beneath the surface, it's a story of God's providence. Providence is God seeing what we need before we need it and providing it or putting everything in place. Before Esther was even born, the people of Israel, God's chosen people, were taken into exile, and God knew that there would be a wicked plot to try to exterminate them. To protect them, God put a plan in place and chose a woman named Hadassah who would execute that plan to save God's people.

Your story is replete with God's providence, too! Before you lost your job, God had a plan in place to provide for you. Before you got sick, your healing had already been arranged. Before that man even thought about leaving you, your future was secured. It may feel like your life is going nowhere, but know that when God has a plan for your life, there may be roadblocks, detours, denials, and setbacks, but the God "who began a good work in you will carry it on to completion" (Philippians 1:6).

Every event and circumstance is used by God to position you for all that God has for you. The Lord works together in all things for the good of those who love God and are called according to God's purpose (Romans 8:28). God never wastes a hurt, disappointment, betrayal, or rejection. What you perceive as a setback is really a setup. God takes messes and makes miracles.

Trust God. Serve God wholeheartedly, and do whatever the Spirit tells you. Give everything God asks for, even when it doesn't make sense to you. We may spend long seasons in waiting, and then, out of nowhere, God will move! People will wonder how you moved so fast, how you got ahead of them. God opens doors no one can shut, positions us in places others will say we have no business being. God will move you out front like God did Esther. God will bless your coming and your going. You may not be able to see or even understand what God is doing. But know that it's a setup!

God set Esther up. When Esther got in to see the king, she immediately won his favor, just as she had with everyone else with whom she had come into contact. During the queen-selection process, a young woman spent the night with the king, and then he sent her back to another part of the harem the next day, where she stayed until he might choose to summon her again. When Esther's turn came to go to the king, he was attracted to her more than any of the other women. He made her queen. It was a divine setup.

Five years later, Haman, one of King Artaxerxes' nobles, was elevated to the number-two position in the kingdom. Everyone was happy for him and honored him by bowing down to him, except Mordecai, who was a faithful Jew and could not give reverence to any human being. Needless to say, this angered Haman, and so he devised a plan to get rid of Mordecai. In fact, Haman decided that he would just wipe out Mordecai's whole race. After convincing the king to comply with his wicked, murderous scheme, Haman prompted Artaxerxes to issue a decree to destroy all the Jews in the kingdom.

When Mordecai heard the decree, he tore his clothes and went into mourning, walking through the city and wailing loudly and bitterly. In fact, there was great mourning among the Jews in every province. Mordecai hoped to capture Esther's attention, and he succeeded—just not in the way he had hoped! First, she just sent new clothes for him to wear. He refused. Then she sent a servant to find out what was troubling him. He sent her word of the decree and urged her to go to the king on behalf of her people. Esther was still less than receptive. She sent a message back to Mordecai that anyone who approached the king in the inner court without being summoned could be put to death. Even she, his wife, could not go before the king uninvited—and he had not summoned her in thirty days. There was nothing she could do, was there?

Get Concerned

You see, Queen Esther sat in the king's house, far removed from her youth as the orphan Hadassah in the home of her compassionate uncle. She had been treated as Persian royalty for five years and more. She was comfortable and safe and apparently oblivious to the gravity of the situation facing her fellow Jews. Why should she be concerned?

Esther's initial response reminds me of some of us as Christians. Now that we are in the house of God, saved and safe, beloved children of our sovereign God, it does not seem to matter to us what is going on in the world, in the nation, in the lives of the people around us. As long as it does not concern me or mine, I'm not concerned with it. As long as I am going to heaven, as long as I and my loved ones are saved, as long as I reap the harvest God promised me, who cares about what happens to the rest of the world?

How quickly we forget that if someone had not been concerned about us, we would still be lost. Yes, some of us have developed spiritual amnesia. We don't read the paper or listen to the news, and when we do, we quickly dismiss what we see and hear as if it doesn't concern us. Like Esther, we are more concerned with maintaining our level of comfort than we are with making sure those who are in need are comforted.

If it doesn't concern you, my sister, then whom should it concern that the health professionals nationwide report that black women have higher rates of HIV/AIDS, high blood pressure, heart disease, stroke, lupus, and breast cancer at young ages—to name just a few?

Somebody somewhere needs to say something! Are we just going to sit idly by while Satan orchestrates the affairs in our world and continually kills, abuses, and destroys our people, our sisters and mothers and aunts and ultimately ourselves? Are we going to live in denial and act like it isn't happening, or if it is, it doesn't concern me? For how long are we going to remain oblivious to the gravity of our own situation and the situations of those around us?

Get in Place

When Esther's words were reported to Mordecai, he sent back this answer:

> "Esther, do not say to yourself that you alone among all the Jews will escape alive.
> For if you keep quiet at such a time as this, help and protection will come to the Jews

from another quarter, but you and your father's family will perish. Yet who knows whether it was not for such a time as this that you were made queen?"

Mordecai let Esther know this wasn't just about her! She had been placed in a royal position at that time to be a blessing. Like her, you have been so positioned at this time to effect change in the world and in the lives of the people around you.

Be clear, however, that you do have choice in the matter. You can choose to remain uninvolved, detached, and silent. But if you remain silent at a time like this, when God has placed you in a position to act, God will use some other means to save God's people, but you may not survive to see that redemption. We are all in this thing together. None of us will be free until all of us are free! It is someone else's child today and yours tomorrow. So, you had better get a grip and do what you can to shut Satan's whole program down.

We have come to this place for such a time as this! You had better know what time it is. Indeed, "for everything there is a season, and a time for every matter under heaven" (verse 3:1). There is "a time to keep silence, and a time to speak" (verse 7).

Some of us have been silent too long. It is time for us to stand up, to speak up and not shut up until we turn things around. We are literally being destroyed one family at a time by poverty, inadequate health care, poor education, substance abuse, and untreated mental illness.

It is not our heritage as African American women to sit idly by while our people are destroyed. All of us have a platform from which to speak, and we have influence. We are in this place today because of uncompromising women, such as Sojourner Truth, Harriet Tubman, Rosa Parks, Fannie Lou Hamer, Shirley Chisholm, Coretta Scott King, Barbara Jordan, Dorothy Height, Maxine Waters, and the millions of unnamed mamas and big mamas, aunties, and cousins whom God positioned to speak up during times of great struggle. They have sacrificed their lives so that we might live abundantly. Take your place in that lineup of the sheroes of our faith!

Get Busy

When it was Esther's moment in time, she decided what she would do. When it is our moment in time, we must decide what we will do. Esther got busy, and so must we. She told Mordecai to gather all the Jews in Susa to fast for three days and nights along with her and her maids. After the three days, she would go to the king. She was willing to lose her life to save the lives of her people. "If I perish, I perish!" she said (Esther 4:17).

Time to Pray

Although unmentioned in the text that allows God's providence to reign without mention of God's name, Esther knew she and her people needed God's strength to fulfill God's mighty call. Esther seemed to know instinctively two key insights that Jesus confided in his disciples centuries later. First, some demons won't be vanquished except through prayer and fasting, and second, there is power when God's people come together and agree in prayer. Esther told Mordecai to call on the Jews to pray and fast as a community. And as in the days of Esther and her people, it is time for us to come together and pray! Through prayer, we can bring down strongholds and demolish addictions. People can be saved, healed, and delivered from anything and everything.

Time to Plan

Once we get prayed up, it's time for us to have a plan! Esther was not just beautiful; she had brains. She did not go to the king with merely an emotional appeal. Rather, she had a strategy already in place. This is no time for us to fall out in weeping and wailing; we can't afford to be dismissed as overemotional or irrational. Lives are at stake, including our own. We must be strategic. We must bide our time. We must take it in stages. And we must seize the opportunities that God provides.

Time to Take a Position

Finally, it's time that we are clear about our positions! It's time for every woman to fulfill her specific assignment. It's time for mothers to be mothers and do whatever is necessary to raise their children in safe environments. It's time for mentors to show young girls what it means to be beautiful and brainy, to use their minds to get them where their body can't. It's time for grandmothers to be grandmothers and help daughters raise their children in the fear and admonition of the Lord. It's time for parents and teachers and politicians to work together toward the quality education of the younger generations. It's time for representatives in Congress, in the Senate, in the state house, and on city councils to rewrite policy to safeguard the lives and quality of life for all.

It's time for all of us to reach out to our sisters and brothers with the good news of Jesus Christ. It's time! It's time! It's time!